SOMETHING TO BE DESIRED
VERONIQUE
VIENNE

E S S A Y S O N D E S I G N

FOREWORD BY OWEN EDWARDS

FOR FABIEN VIENNE

Acknowledgments:

Drawing up a list of the people who have helped me define my point of view turned out to be a daunting task. So many design professionals have been generous, insightful, and inspiring. First and foremost, I am grateful to those who encouraged me to write about the design culture in spite of the fact that I was obviously a dilettante: Steven Heller, D.K. Holland, Susan Szenasy, Martin C. Pedersen, Rick Poynor, Owen Edwards, Frank Zachary, Betsy Pochoda, Jeffrey Klein, Roger Lipsey, and Carl Lehmann-Haupt. I also want to thank editors, mentors, advisors, and publishers who have invested considerable time and resources to help me shape these essays: Helen Pratt, B. Martin Pedersen, Anne Telford, Horace Havemeyer III, Richard Grefé, Jack Crager, Leslie Sherr, Juanita Dugdale, Peggy Roalf, Janet Rumble, Jamie Reynolds, Andrea Birnbaum, Seamus Mullarkey, and Linda Bradford. I am also indebted to friends, acquaintances, colleagues, and role models whose ideas, criticisms, and humor have informed my love of design: Milton Glaser, Peter Blake, Michael Bierut, Stephen Doyle, Marc Gobé, Ken Carbone, Alexander Liberman, Seymour Chwast, Lloyd Ziff, Paul and Myrna Davis, Paula Scher, Robert Priest, Will Hopkins, Mary K. Baumann, Bride Whelan, Moira Cullen, Lorraine Wild, Scott Santoro, Michael Hoffman, Pierre Bernard, Xavier Ross, Cheryl Swanson, Ward Schumaker—and my husband, Bill Young.

Cover photograph by Jeanne Lipsey; design by B. Martin Pedersen and Lauren Slutsky

CONTENTS

CONTENTS

Véronique Vienne is a rare hybrid. Like the mythical creature described by Woody Allen as having "the head of a lion and the body of a lion…but not the same lion," she is a subtle and fascinating amalgam of different careers and different cultures. To put it far too simply, Vienne is a French magazine art director who has reinvented herself as an American writer. To an abundantly Parisian style she has grafted a curiosity, openness, and flexibility that are characteristically New World. In the eloquent manner of an Alistair Cooke, she has become a native *étrangère*. With her two selves seamlessly joined (the seams don't show, at least), she makes a very compelling lion.

I first encountered Véronique in her still more-or-less intact French art director incarnation when I hired her to be the designer of a magazine I was putting together in San Francisco. We interviewed one another at lunch in a very good restaurant, which, since I was new in town, she had chosen. It was the first of many choices that seemed always to be right on target. As the coffee arrived, I offered Véronique the job, though I'd made up my mind about two minutes after she sat down. My instincts told me this would be a person who would be wonderful to have around, whether the magazine succeeded or failed (it succeeded, in no small part due to her). At the time, she was writing for Bay Area publications, though she was not yet officially a writer. I offered little encouragement, on the jealous theory that there were more than enough writers as it was. But her affinity for—and pleasure in—words in English made her one of those increasingly rare art directors with an editor's instincts, able to use design, and the talents of photographers and illustrators, to take readers in unexpected directions.

When Véronique moved to New York, where she had started out in this country, she took an art directorial job at a big magazine; but she was already looking suspiciously like a writer, doing essays on a wide spectrum of subjects for an eclectic array of magazines. Now, several years later, the transformation is complete: With a number of successful books to her credit,

Vienne is a bona fide member of the ink-stained trade. But she remains fascinated by design of all sorts, whether of the things around us or the schemes that make us want those things or in how the mysterious concept of Good Design shapes (or misshapes) our lives in subtle and not-so-subtle ways.

This wry hybrid brings a particularly appealing combination of European scholarship and American cheekiness to bear on the complex interplay of mind, material, and marketing that dominates modern life in the U.S. and its empire of conquering brands. Though steeped in our culture, she doesn't see things as we do. Her determination to analyze and understand almost everything has the inexhaustible quality of a smoky conversation at the Café de Flore, while her quirky responses to everyday life are right out of some paranoid New York comic's monologue. For instance, her dubious take on chairs: "As far as I am concerned, when you sit in a chair, people are likely to fire you, reprimand you, or even worse, lecture you." And I somehow doubt that any purely American thinker would be likely to see Mickey Mouse and Michael Jackson as blood brothers, "split between a black and a white identity."

When I failed to show much enthusiasm for Vienne's quest to become a writer, it was for entirely selfish reasons; what I needed was a talented art director, not more competition in the words-for-dollars scrum. Luckily for us, she did not wait for my encouragement, nor heed whatever muttered warnings I offered. She went right ahead, Frankishly stubborn, Yankishly confident. Now we can delight in what she has become, a truly original observer of the hearts of our matter and manner.

If I was not inclined to mentor, apparently I could not resist giving a little gratuitous advice. Upon reading one of her early essays, she remembers me saying, "You're trying too hard to be interesting. Don't be afraid to bore people." Odd advice, perhaps, but at least the right parts of it stuck. Véronique Vienne isn't afraid. And she certainly isn't boring.

—*Owen Edwards*

A reevaluation of the Situationist thesis
More than 40 years ago in Paris,
an obscure group of cultural critics who
called themselves "Situationists" began
protesting against the escalating
commercial takeover of everyday life.

Mesmerized by the computer or television screen, most of us are docile spectators in much of our life, our idle hands forever deprived of the tactile satisfaction of actually making things. This enforced passivity has dire consequences for the brain. Our hands are connected to our gray matter by a crisscrossing network of nerve pathways that travel back and forth from the right brain to the left hand and from left brain to the right hand. There is evidence that toolmaking is linked to the development of language. Recent studies on the mind-body connection suggest that the development (or atrophy, as the case may be) of parts of the body can in turn affect corresponding parts of the brain. So, while manual dexterity stimulates our central nervous system, simple spectatorship has a tendency to numb the mind.

With nothing to fabricate, the majority of people are reduced to buying ready-made products—examining them, poking them, and fondling them in the process just to satisfy the yearning in their fingers. Shopping is a substitute for producing. When my daughter was a teenager, she would often say, like so many of her contemporaries, "Mom, I have nothing to do. I'm bored. Let's go shopping!" It soon became a family joke. We worked out a couple of silly variations, including, "Mom, my closet is full of clothes. I have nothing to wear. Let's go shopping," and "Mom, I have too many pairs of sneakers. I am confused. Let's go shopping."

From time to time, I indulged her shopping impulses, but I also suggested fun alternatives: fix toys, repaint the bathroom, make jam, wax the furniture. One of her favorite mood-uppers, it turned out, was doing the silver. I will always cherish the memory of her sitting at the kitchen table, a big apron secured around her chest, happily polishing our odd collection of forks and spoons.

"In his or her day-dreams the passive worker becomes an active consumer," wrote John Berger, Britain's eminent critic and novelist, in his 1972 best-seller *Ways of Seeing.* Acquiring things, Berger believes, is a poor substitute for fashioning objects. The spectator-self, no longer involved with the making of artifacts, envies the consumer-self, who gets to touch and use new gadgets, appliances, devices, and goods. Deprived of the sensual pleasure of manual creation, we satisfy our tactile cravings by purchasing more and more ready-made objects and products.

This perception is not new. More than 40 years ago in Paris, an obscure group of cultural critics who called themselves "Situationists" began protesting against the escalating commercial takeover of everyday life, and against the artists, illustrators, photographers, art directors, and graphic designers who manufactured this fake gee-whiz reality. In his book *The Society of Spectacle*, French Situationist leader Guy Debord wrote, "In our society, where modern conditions of production prevail, all of life presents itself as an immense accumulation of spectacles." Yet by today's standards, the spectacle hadn't even begun. This was before the Cuban revolution, before the invasion of Tibet, before the Pill, before *La Dolce Vita*, before Pop Art. In the 1958 Paris of the early Situationists, Edith Piaf was singing "Milord," François Truffaut was shooting *The 400 Blows*, and demure Danish Modern was the cutting edge.

With a clairvoyance that's startling in hindsight, the short-lived Situationist International movement (1957–1972) predicted our most serious current predicament: According to recent findings, we spend 58 percent of our waking time interacting with the media; people sleep less and spend less time with their family in order to watch more television; megaplexes and superstores are increasingly designed to resemble theme parks; and the Mall of America in Minneapolis hosts more visitors than Disney World, Disneyland, and the Grand Canyon combined. In his 1999 book *The Entertainment Economy: How Mega-Media Forces Are Transforming Our Lives*, Michael J. Wolf asserts: "We have come to expect that we will be entertained all the time. Products and brands that deliver on this expectation are succeeding. Products that do not will disappear."

No wonder the Situationists' ethos has become the mantra of critics and detractors of our imagineering culture. Everyone who is anyone these days is dropping their name—from *Adbusters* and *Emigré* to Greil Marcus and J. Abbott Miller. Debord's seminal book, *The Society of Spectacle*, is on the list of the trendy Zone Books, and MIT Press published *The Situationist City* in 1998, a comprehensive investigation of the Situationists' urbanist theories, written by Simon Sadler. Move over, Paul Virillio—SI, as the Situationist International movement is now known, is back as the latest French intellectual import.

An underground movement that shunned the limelight—the members of this elusive group lived by the precepts they preached—SI's subversive ideology at first defies comprehension. Unless you understand the specific context of the period, many of their assertions make little sense today. Influenced by Lettrist International, a radical group of the 1950s that sought to revitalize urban life through the fusion of poetry and music, Debord and his colleague Raoul Vaneigem used Dadaist slogans to spread their message. "The more you consume, the less you live," and "Be realistic, demand the impossible," are two of the most memorable SI pronouncements.

Despite its so-called anarchist mentality, the SI methodology was precisely constructed. The name of the group was born out of the realization that participants had to create in their everyday life special conditions—special "situations"—in order to resist the insidious appeal of the pseudo-needs of increased consumption and to overcome the mounting sense of alienation that has characterized the postmodern age. They conducted open-ended experiments that involved playful constructive behavior aimed at scrambling mental expectations. Most popular of these strategies: taking aimless strolls through a busy neighborhood, deliberately rearranging the furniture in their apartments to create as many obstacles as possible, systematically rejecting labor-saving devices, and voluntarily disorienting themselves by consulting the map of London when visiting Amsterdam. Called "drifting"—*dérive* in French—the technique was an effective way to "reclaim the night," to momentarily defy the white patriarchy of traditional space/time.

Like most rational people today, I would find this approach naïve and dogmatic if I hadn't experienced it firsthand. In 1960, as a student at the Paris Beaux-Arts school of architecture, I was unwittingly part of an SI experiment. The very first day I showed up at the studio with a dozen other new recruits, the instructor announced that we should reconvene at *La Palette*, a bistro across the street. At nine in the morning, the sidewalk had just been washed and the waiter was trundling the cast-iron tables out in the open. We each grabbed a wicker chair from a tall stack in a corner, picked our spot on the terrace, angled our seats to catch the morning sun, stretched our legs, yawned, and ordered a round of black coffee.

"This is your first lesson in architecture," said the instructor, a gaunt young man in a black turtleneck—the trademark look of the avant-garde back then. "For the next three months, we will spend six hours a day sitting right here. I want you to learn about space/time—particularly how to use space in order to waste time. Unless you understand that, you'll never be good architects."

I now know that this was straightforward SI doctrine. Embracing Arthur Rimbaud's assertion that laziness is a refusal to compartmentalize time, Situationists advocated "living without restrictions or dead time," and "never work—never risk dying of boredom." They wasted time deliberately—and playfully—as a guerrilla tactic to combat the sense of emptiness imposed by the relentless spectacle of consumption that was quickly engulfing French culture.

And so, for the first semester, we sat at the bistro from nine in the morning until three in the afternoon, five days a week. Except for mornings when we would drift through Paris, sketchpads in hand, making detailed drawings of whatever caught our fancy—a stairway leading to the riverbank, an abandoned gazebo in a park, the monumental gate of a hospital—you would find us huddled at the terrace of *La Palette*. This was *in situ* urban anthropology. I learned to observe how people choose the best spot to sit, how lovers fight, how couples brood, how friends compete, how everyone sits straighter when a pretty girl walks in, how people celebrate on payday, and how they scrutinize a menu when they are broke.

Sometimes we students would talk, sometimes we would draw, sometimes we would read, sometimes we would argue. Often we would simply daydream. As promised, the space/time equation became a reality, one rich in surprises and discoveries. We became familiar with the angles of the various streets, the movements of the sun, the sounds of the city, the rhythm of life around us. No two minutes were ever alike. As we sat there, absorbing what felt like vital information, we developed a perception of the human scale—a critical notion for architects. And then, almost reluctantly, after lunch, we drifted across the street to the studio where we worked late into the night to acquire the rudiments of the classical orders of architecture.

I never completed my architectural studies. Instead, I moved to the States and eventually became a magazine art director. During my career in design, I often used the *dérive* technique to avoid the pitfalls of linear thinking. Instead of focusing on a thorny design conundrum, the solution would come to me unsolicited if I patiently listened to a photographer rant on about his midlife crisis, or when I watched a five-year-old play with her baby brother. Another Situationist construct also came in handy. Called *détournement*, translated as "rerouting," it consists of transforming images by interpreting them to mean something of your own making. SI theorists liked to describe the method as "hijacking, misappropriation, corruption of pre-existing aesthetic elements." I simply call it sticking words on top of images.

Rerouting images is the basic modus operandi of graphic communication. The minute you caption a photograph, or place a headline next to a picture, create a collage, single out a pull-quote, or write cover lines, you subvert the significance of both word and image. I believe that most of the creative tensions between editors and art directors, and between clients and designers, evolve from a misunderstanding of how visual artifacts can be reconfigured into constructed situations.

Chris Dixon, art director of *Adbusters* magazine, a Vancouver-based anti-consumerism publication that has whole-heartedly embraced the SI legacy, is probably one of the few North American designers who consciously uses *détournement*. "Often the captions we use in the magazine are much more provocative than the images themselves," he says. "In fact, we deliberately use rather conventional photographs to let our readers know that we speak the same language they do." Even though its overall message is anti-commercial and anti-advertising, *Adbusters* is surprisingly well-designed, as if to mock the very aesthetic that drives the advertising community.

Where *Adbusters* and SI part ways is on the discourse they have chosen to promote similar ideas. "We link anti-consumerism to the environmental movement," explains Dixon. "Readers understand the correlation between buying too many useless products and depleting the natural resources of the planet." Concern for the environment never appears in the newspapers, journals, graffiti, or manifestos left behind by the SI. They didn't have much of a social agenda either. Their mandate was to resist the cultural imperialism that drains human beings of that most French of concepts, their *joie de vivre*. Boredom was their enemy; happiness their goal. Another of their maxims was: "They are buying your happiness—steal it back."

The Situationist idea of happiness is very different from the "hedonomics" of the buying experience, as defined by Wolf in *The Entertainment Economy*. Whereas Americans equate feeling good with having "fun," the French in general, and the SI in particular, describe happiness as liberating—euphoric, mischievous, prankish. It's the feeling that swept over France during the first weeks of the May 1968 general strike, when much of Paris took to the streets in what seemed at first more a carnival than a student revolt.

The Situationists were responsible for initiating the construction of barricades in the streets of Paris that month. Pull up some cobblestones, add a half-dozen trash cans, more cobblestones, some discarded lumber, maybe a broken bicycle. Borrow chairs from a café, sit, and wait. They also encouraged students to cover the walls of the city with Lettrist-inspired graffiti ("It is forbidden to forbid"). Last but not least, they were credited with giving the rebellion its upbeat and high-spirited signature.

But the events of 1968—not only in France but all over the world—were eventually "rerouted" by the Establishment. As Thomas Frank, editor-in-chief of *The Baffler*, explains in his 1997 book *The Conquest of Cool*, the anti-consumerism rebellion of the postwar era was commodified by the ad agencies of Madison Avenue into what is now known as the "Youth Culture"—one of the greatest marketing tools of the twentieth century. The Society of Spectacle was here to stay. Blaming themselves for their failure to change society, but also grieving for the millions of consumers who would experience euphoria only through shopping, Debord and his troops dispersed in 1972. Their ideas, however, continued to resonate, quite notably in the early days of English punk (Jamie Reid's photo-collage for the Sex Pistols captured the defiant challenge punk rock posed to class and authority). Tragically unable to recapture the *joie de vivre* of the early days of SI, Debord took his own life in December 1994.

Five years later, events would prove that the spirit he had championed still survives. On December 5, 1999, the front page of *The New York Times* featured a photograph that would have cheered him up. Taken by Jimi Lott of *The Seattle Times*, it showed Mr. and Mrs. Santa Claus being escorted home by four riot policemen, the cops wearing Ninja-Turtle combat boots and padded breastplates. The violent protests against the World Trade Organization in Seattle had so disrupted holiday shopping, explained the caption, that the Yuletide pair had to be put under police protection.

As one flipped through the newspaper, one quickly realized that the former Saint Nicholas (a historical figure recast in 1931 in red and white by Coca-Cola as the beloved icon we now identify with Christmas shopping) was not the only consumer icon that needed police protection. Riot troops had been posted in front of all the retail stores in downtown Seattle—guarding Starbucks, Banana Republic, Coach, The Gap, and Gucci, to name just a few. The entrance to Niketown, in particular, looked like a *Star Wars* set, with hooded figures in black armor standing at attention, their four-foot truncheons poised to strike.

It looked like the police were confronting rowdy crowds not to protect civil liberties and political institutions—but to protect global brands. Though one didn't have to be a trend forecaster to feel that brand backlash was coming ("My wish for the New Year was to get through meetings without someone mentioning branding," joked renowned Web page editorial designer Jessica Hefland shortly after), most of us never expected it would be so sudden, so graphic, or so ready-for-prime-time television. "The revolution will not be televised," sang Gil Scott-Heron in 1974. Wishful thinking. The anti-consumerism, anti-brand revolution, complete with demonstrators smashing store windows, was on the eleven o'clock news. Over and over, the same scenes were aired every few minutes, as if to "brand" the violent images in the minds of viewers.

Kalle Lasn, editor of *Adbusters* magazine and famous for advocating what he calls "culture jamming," was one of the few people who wasn't surprised by the Seattle uproar. In fact, the December '99 issue of his magazine had an article predicting that the WTO conference would be "a historic confrontation between civil society and corporate rule." His book, *Culture*

Jam, The Uncooling of America, had just been released. *Time* magazine had praised him for taking arms against our 3,000-marketing-messages-a-day society. Still, he wasn't prepared for what he saw when he went to Seattle to observe the riots.

"It was like a festival," he says. "Except for a few people confronting cops, demonstrators were laid-back, happy, having fun. There was a lot of street theater, spontaneous happenings, and cheerful pranks being played." It had a Situationist ambiance, for sure. But then, unexpectedly, Lasn got his first whiff of teargas. "I'll never forget that smell," he says. "Nor will I forget the savage look on the faces of the policemen. They really didn't get it."

Who *does* get it? And why do we see global brands as a threat to our very existence—a threat so real it galvanized 30,000 people to take to the streets? "There were more than 100 different groups," says Lasn. "Environmentalists, students, anarchists, but also musty old socialists, Christians tired of the violence on TV, critics of genetic engineering, and card-carrying union members—every single one of them worried about some unofficial global government body enforcing an elite corporate agenda."

That same week, for the fifth anniversary of Debord's death, I had given my graphic design students at the School of Visual Arts a series of *dérive* exercises directly inspired by my own SI experience and studies. First they had to draw a map of all their travels/wanderings/whereabouts in New York City during the last three months, plotting on paper their perception of time/space in the Big Apple. Their map, I told them, was supposed to be an "aid to reverie," a tool for bringing their private space into the public sphere. Then, they had to explore and draw the Beaux-Arts colonnade at the Manhattan Bridge anchorage, with the idea that urbanism was in fact "the organization of silence."

Though the discussions, laughter, confessions, and astute comments generated by my students as we reviewed their serendipitous maps and awkward sketches reaffirmed my faith in design and art education, I am not sure they really got it. How could they? Unlike my instructor in Paris 40 years ago, I couldn't ask my MFA students to spend a whole semester observing the sidewalk. My education at the government-sponsored Beaux-Arts school of architecture had been free, whereas in contrast, theirs was expensive. To pay for their hefty tuition, my students had worked overtime, gone into debt, or impoverished themselves. And here came the final irony, the ultimate sign of how prescient the Situationists had been and how eerily relevant they remain: I was keenly aware that I couldn't squander my students' money—they were consumers of a knowledge that I was trying to share with them—and as a result, my class itself had to be a spectacle of sorts, not the powerful and lasting experience gained by the subversion of spectacle.

How MoMA turned design into a marketing device
What's the origin of our obsession with
"good design?" Why does Modernism
position itself above the realm of human frailties?
And is the high moral ground detrimental
to our profession?

Design competitions are invitations to partake in intimidating rituals of assessment and rejection. We feel compelled to respond to calls for entries to seek the approval of our peers—despite the fact that, pressed for time, the various judges often know very little about the projects they are supposed to evaluate. Ultimately, we abide by their impromptu verdict to define what's good and what's bad design. *Jury*-rigged, indeed. their awards nonetheless set the standards of excellence for our profession.

This behavior is unique to designers. Though other creative types, decorators and writers for example, also have their competitions—their games and tournaments—being "good" is never the main issue. Brilliance, originality, proficiency—this is what matters. These artists don't have to stand on a high moral ground to get validation from their peers. Unlike us, they can be "bad"—and still get a standing ovation.

Designers developed this strange do-good dependency in the early 1950s, when the modern design movement was still in its infancy. For five years, between 1950 and 1955, they were subjected to a grueling evaluation exercise sponsored by the highest authority in the field—New York's Museum of Modern Art, or MoMA for short. In collaboration with the Chicago Merchandise Mart, the museum developed one of the most ambitious competition agendas to date—the prestigious Good Design program.

Reading about this amazing postwar brainwashing campaign is an eye-opener. Most informative is a short essay on the subject, written in 1994 by Terence Riley, chief curator of Design and Architecture at MoMA, and Edward Eigen, an advanced student at MIT. Part of a series of studies on the role of the museum at midcentury, the well-documented article, entitled "Between the Museum and the Marketplace: Selling Good Design," explains in great detail how the design community was systematically and deliberately conditioned to equate Modernism with good design—and good design with good business.

Indeed, the Good Design story is steeped in Modernist romance. The idea was the brain child of Edgar Kaufmann Jr., son of the Pittsburgh department store magnate who commissioned Frank Lloyd Wright's Fallingwater masterpiece in Mill Run, Pennsylvania. In 1946, the younger Kaufmann, then in his thirties, was appointed director of MoMA's Department of Industrial Design. A proponent of the arts—he had studied painting in Vienna, typography in Florence, and architecture at Wright's Taliesen Foundation—he turned out to be a marketing genius ahead of his time. Trained in his father's store, he orchestrated the Good Design exhibitions with the enthusiasm and optimism of a retailer.

The originality of his scheme was to turn a curatorial feat into an unprecedented and well-coordinated merchandising and media event. His goal was ambitious: stimulate the postwar economy by convincing the American people to buy new products—presumably because these late-model products were better than old ones.

The five-year program consisted of three exhibitions a year, each displaying between 200 and 400 objects. The shows presented a comprehensive selection of what Kaufmann and his juries believed to be the best examples of modern products designed during that period. One of the distinguishing features of the program was its taxonomy: Instead of presenting gold, silver, and bronze medals as well as prizes, a practice popularized by international exhibitions in the late nineteenth century, the jurors awarded only an unassailable Good Design stamp of approval. This democratic system of classification allowed the jurists to dodge the difficult issue of defining by what standards they were assessing each entry. Warm and fuzzy, with its aura of wholesomeness, the word "good" was assumed to be above the realm of human frailties. To this day, "good design" is a lofty concept that evades definition.

Back then, arbitrary and unqualified pronouncements by

patrons and pundits went unchallenged. Case in point, the "Great Ideas of Western Man" campaign launched in 1950 by Chicago industrialist Walter P. Paepcke, the enlightened advocate of Modernism who founded the Container Corporation of America and the Aspen Design Conference. Still hailed as one of the greatest advertising coups of all times, the Container Corporation's institutional campaign celebrated the concept of justice and liberty as defined by the likes of Alexander Hamilton and Theodore Roosevelt. In the perspective of today's political correctness, Paepcke's white-male-establishment point of view would probably come under attack. So would Kaufmann's somewhat capricious definition of goodness or the overt commercialism of his MoMA-sponsored Good Design venture. But those were innocent times.

Good Design exhibition catalogues were, after all, explicit service guides, listing the objects on display, their price, and where they could be purchased. The installations were designed by celebrated architects and designers—Charles and Ray Eames and Paul Rudolph among them—and were laid out like department stores, with housewares, accessories, wallcoverings, furniture, appliances, and linens featured in separate areas. The artists' visions were systematically de-emphasized: The objects alone were the stars. To further reinforce the authenticity of the program, the products selected by MoMA were awarded bold and distinctive "Good Design" tags, easily identifiable from a distance when displayed in a busy retail environment.

The first two shows of each year were held in Chicago at the Merchandise Mart during the winter and summer housewares market. The third, timed to coincide with the Christmas buying season, was held in New York at the Museum of Modern Art. A two-month-long media blitz, the holiday promotional extravaganza was supported by carefully synchronized magazine and newspaper articles, symposia, advertising, consumer opinion polls, radio interviews, and television appearances by Kaufmann. In 1954, MoMA even developed a Good Design game show format for TV.

Good Design's synergy between education and consumption was irresistible. At the time, you had to be a curmudgeon not to applaud its success. Architect Philip Johnson was one of Kaufmann's few antagonists. Elitist by nature, the architect of the Glass House was annoyed by the Good Design program's populist approach—and by Kaufmann's evident endorsement of Frank Lloyd Wright's pragmatic philosophy. But there was more to Johnson's uneasiness than just rivalry. He believed that only a formal definition of Modernism could "end the divorce between industry and culture," whereas Kaufmann preferred to keep things vague, professing no apparent ideology— "no ax to grind." For Kaufmann, Good Design was a euphoric concept that equated aesthetics with "eye appeal" and newness with innovation. His only bias was against decorative vocabulary borrowed from the past. He made no distinction between machine-made or handcrafted objects and only excluded from consideration things that were not readily available on the U.S. market.

As it turned out, Good Design's domesticated form of Modernism was fraught with subliminal messages—some of which we are still trying to decipher today. Back then, the word *good* was linked with the notion of ethics and morality. Milton Glaser remembers how, in the early 1950s, "*Good* made reference to things that were supposed to be honest and truthful, like, for example, Abstract Art. In contrast, today, *good* has no moral, spiritual, or redemptive agenda. *Good* simply means effective. *Good* means that which sells." For him, as for an increasing number of designers, the idea that problem-solving, in and of itself, is enough to generate good design is wearing thin.

In "Design and Business—The War Is Over," an article published in 1995 in the AIGA Journal, Glaser elaborates on why he believes the design community got shortchanged in the struggle between commerce and culture. "In the United States, the social impulses that characterized Bauhaus thought began to be transformed by our pragmatic objectives, such as the use of design as a marketing tool and the elevation of style and taste as the moral center of design," he writes. "It occurred so swiftly that none of us was quite prepared for it."

Another witness to the period, ceramist Eva Zeisel, who won countless Good Design awards for her elegant and witty design crockery, challenges the very assumption that good design gave products a marketing advantage. "Good Design was never good business," says the spirited artist, now in her nineties. "It only appealed to a very narrow elite. For the majority of Americans, it was O.K. to have modern appliances in the kitchen—but in the rest of the house, particularly in the living room, traditional styles prevailed." She maintains that what Kaufmann called Good Design was nothing more than lack of applied ornamentation. Milton Glaser would agree: "Good Design stood for the elimination of storytelling," he now says.

Kaufmann was a staunch Modernist who conducted a one-man campaign against what he sincerely believed to be the "bad" taste of the public. In his own words, he wanted to see "a more extensive repertory of shapes, textures, and above all, surface patterns not imitative of the past." He held a highly publicized panel discussion at MoMA on the subject, "Is Ornament Good Design?"

Zeisel remembers with a chuckle that she was one of the panelists. Though her work was never overly decorative, she was not a relentless purist. After viewing one of the Good Design shows, she wrote, "Nothing could be said to have been made for glory, or for the admiration of the people. There were no lapis lazuli glazes, no silver-colored pottery, no sumptuous yellow tiles. Dishes were white, with severe, straight sides... The call to reduce sounded almost as if calling out to us sinners to repent, repent, repent... Why not call out rejoice, rejoice, rejoice?"

Postmodernism can be interpreted as a gallant attempt to bring joy back into the design process. It did succeed up to a point, but it didn't release us from nagging assumptions about

WHAT'S BAD ABOUT GOOD DESIGN?

"good" and "bad" design. Its over-the-top historicism didn't help us sort out the difference between what's modern and what's dated. Its wasteful eclecticism didn't promote a new understanding of the role of ornamentation. Most disturbing, postmodernism never challenged the notion that the measure of excellence of a design solution is its commercial success.

Today, good design is touted as the one advantage that gives products their competitive edge—like Philippe Starck's whimsical flyswatter and Michael Graves' translucent toilet brush. In our economy, Modernist-inspired styling is the differential that matters at the cash register. At long last, Edgar Kaufmann's vision is a reality. But beware: the reality may not be timeless! Back at MoMA, a number of objects from the 3,000-piece prestigious Design collection are decaying, quite literally. Plastic bowls are collapsing into toxic blobs. Foam cushions are turning into sand. Acrylic parts are becoming an unruly mess. Nothing can be done to reverse this natural process. Made of experimental "fugitive" plastics, rubbers, or foams, the elegant artifacts of the midcentury era are fading, melting, crumbling, and stiffening in their display cases. That the objects—and not the sensibilities behind them—have suffered worse for time is most fitting. In our age of obsolescence, disintegration isn't necessarily a "bad" thing. All "good" things, the saying goes, must come to an end.

Wayfinding as the defining experience
Navigating a store is like negotiating our
collective assumptions about who we think
we are and who we would like to be.

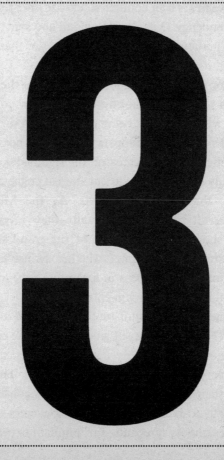

As soon as you walk into a store, your attention drifts to the right. Even left-handed people like me can't help but glance starboard. It's instinctive. You always make a beeline for whatever happens to be on the right side as you walk in. No matter what it is—a pile of cashmere sweaters or a special on umbrellas—it gets your attention.

Knowing this, merchants bait their customers with nothing short of dexterity—a word that comes from the Latin *dexter*, meaning "to the right." Nature or nurture? Retailers have always noticed that the right side, which is, coincidentally, the creative, nonverbal side of the brain, is more conducive to impulse buying. Well-established cultural conventions that favor clockwise movements over counter-clockwise ones reinforce this neurological tendency. Outside of England and some of her former colonies, making a right turn is a lot easier than making a left turn.

The trick for merchandising experts is to find the exact spot in a store (not too close to the entrance, but not too far inside) where people will go without being prompted. In the New York Bloomingdale's flagship, shoppers love to wander aimlessly among cosmetic counters located on the right side of the main aisle. At Tiffany's, they can't help but stare at engagement rings. At the Gap, they size up T-shirts. At the Metropolitan Museum—the ultimate cultural mall—they investigate the crowded gift shop on the right side of the grand staircase. In almost every store in this country, whether exclusive or not, the bulk of the foot traffic happens in a comfort zone located on a fuzzy diagonal right of the main entrance.

Does this mean that the stuff on the left side of a store is left to gather dust? No way. The left side becomes the right side as soon as you turn around. This is where retailers catch empty-handed shoppers on their way out of the store. There, on the right side of their escape route, these sluggish consumers must tangle with hats, scarves, sunglasses, and souvenirs—spoils that will turn their fruitless spree into a triumphant expedition.

All that people need to navigate retail mazes is the foolproof compass of their peripheral vision. They can cross the main selling floor, ride up and down escalators, and find the right merchandise at the right price without ever having to know where they are going—or why. In retail dreamland, wayfinding is a no-brainer. It's meant to be that way; the more you have to think, the less likely you are to use your credit card.

To favor right-brain receptivity over left-brain linear thinking, in-store navigational information is transmitted through the senses. We perceive ceiling heights, smells, sounds, temperature changes, lights, and shadows, and take our cues from them. For example, from the corner of your eye you notice a brightly illuminated area, somewhere ahead and slightly to the right. You know, without having to be told, that you'll find stuff there for less than $99. Behind the escalators, muffled classical music tells you that you're approaching the men's store—it's time to think leather accessories and spicy colognes. Beyond the watch department, thick carpeting slows you down. This is a restricted area; you've probably wandered by mistake into the fine jewelry department.

Walking into and through a store is the closest thing to appreciating what it's like to be legally blind. Retailscapes are laid out in such a way as to discourage visual scrutiny while encouraging total body awareness and open-ended, head-to-toe receptivity. They map out the emotional territory of the shopping experience, emphasizing its main throughways, busy intersections, quiet shortcuts, and hidden rest stops. They are designed to shut out the rational mind and help shoppers get in touch with their creative side.

That's why cosmetics products are sold near the main entrance—with the hottest vendors stationed on the right side. Buoyant color palettes and glittering mirrors, brushes, testers, jars, and bottles make these beauty counters look like artists' studios. From this alluring gateway, shoppers are inspired to proceed upward into a right-brain world ruled by artists, stylists, designers, and arbiters of elegance. As you rise up from floor to floor, the taste level of the decor rises with you. Chandeliers replace recessed lighting. Aisles get wider. Noise reverberation diminishes. Merchandise is getting sparse. Greater opulence is implied by a process of elimination. You know that you've reached the store's luxurious inner sanctum when the only signs of exuberance are the over-the-top figures on the price tags.

Distracted sleepwalkers are in for an unpleasant surprise when they venture beyond these couture salons on the proverbial third floor. In most department stores, the upper levels are no longer encouraging people to wander in a hypnotic trance. Instead, it's time to wake up for a little comparative shopping. At about 100 feet above ground, visual clues prompt shoppers to switch from right brain to left brain. The colors are lighter, the hallways narrower and the racks more numerous. Here, the merchandising strategy promotes frantic bargain hunting. You are urged now to investigate things counter-clockwise—against the grain. Winter coats on sale are on the other side of the aisle, while close-out comforters are behind you on the left side. At this altitude, you're forced to read directional signage: stark billboards with bold prices and loud percentage signs.

Navigating a store is like negotiating our collective assumptions about who we think we are and who we would like to be. People choose stores for their merchandise, but also for their special geography. Where things are displayed is more telling than the way they are displayed. In Barneys original flagship in New York's Chelsea district, women used to walk through the men's department to get to their section—almost as if they had to sneak behind men's backs to buy a couple of deliciously frivolous garments. At Barnes & Noble bookstores, espresso bars are strategically located on a mezzanine, and there is ample dead space for bookworms to nibble on their literary finds. In the Chanel megastore on 57th Street in New York, shoes are sold at the bottom of a soaring grand staircase—the very spot where Cinderella lost her glass slipper.

Staunch consumerism is dead. Today, the most rewarding buying sprees are compelling mythical journeys. That's why smart shoppers don't shop for things, they shop for locations. They may not know what to buy, but they know where to find it. The rack on the right side of the Ralph Lauren boutique at Bergdorf Goodman. The nook at the bottom of the escalator at Brooks Brothers. The first display table as you walk into the Discovery Store in Grand Central Terminal.

Where?—not What? or How much?—is the question they ask themselves as they adjust their internal compass. They realize that successful retailers don't sell products as much as create destinations on invisible maps. A skilled shopper knows the way to the best spots.

Branding the metric system
*The great originality of the metric system
was its pageantry. By creating a ritual
object, its inventors stumbled by chance
upon a modern idea—create a
popular icon to symbolize a brand.*

One-meter-point-seven-two. I was tall for a French woman. But when I moved to the U.S., I lost my advantage. Everything—and everyone—was so much taller, larger, bolder. America, I figured, had been conceived on a different scale. Immigrants don't translate; they convert. Overnight I shed my metric size and gladly exchanged my 172 centimeters for a five-foot-nine-inch frame.

The metric system was introduced in Europe by the French at the end of the French Revolution, inspired by an ancient Hindu-Arabic decimal system. Its counterpart, the U.S. customary system (also called a duodecimal system), is a fossilized holdover from the British Empire. The main difference between the two systems is philosophical—the metric system is based on the number 10, the U.S. system is based on 12.

A ten-system versus a twelve-system is like digital versus analog. Two languages, two cultures. Customary-12 bespeaks the cycles of nature—12 hours, 12 months, 12 constellations of the zodiac. When opting for the decimal system, French scientists were trying to choose the most democratic common denominator—the ten digits of the human hand.

The mathematical properties of number 10 and number 12 further characterize each system. In addition to itself and 1, each number offers differing divisors: 10 can be divided only by 2 and 5, while 12 offers twice as many division options: 2, 3, 4, and 6. As a result, the French system promotes small incremental subdivisions, while the old British system is most amenable to fractions.

Coming to America for me meant learning my fractions. In the land of the brave and the free, three-quarters feels heftier than 0.75. To use the new system efficiently, I learned to estimate quarters, thirds, eighths, and sixteenths. I figured that, in a country built by peripatetic pioneers, pilgrims, wanderers, and go-getters, one must be able to make rough fractional guesses, shoot from the hip, and measure distances by simply pacing around.

Unlike freewheeling computations between inches, feet, and yards that unceremoniously shift the units of measure from 16 to 12 to 3, metric operations are predicated upon a unique consistent dimension. The meter is at the apex of the French decimal system. It is not a concept, but a thing—an actual platinum stick hermetically sealed in a vault in a museum located in the chic Parisian suburb of Sèvres. A national relic, it was never put on display, its invisible yet glowing presence forever a living mystery. As a kid, I remember being told how all our measurements—the width of the Boulevard Saint Germain, the length of the latest Dior skirt, the height of the Eiffel Tower, and the diameter of the tarte Tatin at the local patisserie—all were made to be measured in terms of this precious buried treasure.

Today, a replica of the metric icon is on display at the Arts et Métiers museum in Paris. French visitors peer into its case with nothing short of awe, the way Americans look at the United States Constitution. With a difference, though. Called the *Mêtre Étalon* (*étalon* means "standard"), the platinum unit has acquired an accidental phallic identity: in French, *étalon* also means stallion. In the minds of French schoolchildren, who are taught at an early age to revere and admire the metric system's beautiful symmetry, the original measuring stick seems endowed with super-manly proportions. It is the generatrix rod—the-size-that-begets-all-sizes, the studhorse of the Sèvres International Bureau of Weights and Measures.

The great originality of the metric system was its pageantry. By creating a ritual object, its inventors stumbled by chance upon a modern idea—create a popular icon to symbolize a brand. A simple and elegantly graduated rule, the meter is a highly marketable gadget. It's the right length—39.37 inches long. Not ostentatious, yet authoritative. Its perfect measurement marks the boundaries between large and small, public and private, architecture and manufacture. Multiplied, it soon acquires a monumental scale; divided, it quickly defines the realm of intimacy. Lightweight, handy, versatile, it can easily be used to determine the maximum length of a drawer, the appropriate height for a workbench, and the most comfortable distance between two strangers.

The meter was designed to be a universal measure, one that would appeal to the greatest possible number of people. Purveyors of revolutionary ideas to the rest of the world, eighteenth-century French scientists and philosophers decided to capitalize on their reputation and create a product that could be exported for a profit. If successful, they figured the metric system would boost the economy by generating countless new jobs for French artisans impoverished by the follies of the revolution. Instruments of measures would have to be manufactured, pamphlets and posters explaining their use would have to be printed, machines would have to be retooled.

In France, there were at the time more than 800 different measures of length, weight, and volume. Incompatible standards with poetic names derived from common objects: ropes, chains, sticks, rods, canes, lashes, pickets, and dowels. Also seeds, grains, kernels, specks, smidgens—even "suspicion" and "scruples." The confusion had been encouraged for centuries by feudal lords who had successfully derailed previous attempts at establishing a coherent numerical system in order to delay the establishment of a centralized power structure.

Getting into the spirit of renewal of the two-year-old revolution, French lawmakers were able to reopen the metric debate in 1791. It took six years of research, evaluations, and scientific experiments for them to redefine the project and position it as an international breakthrough rather than a national priority. Two astronomers, Méchain and Delambre, were said to have calculated the distance from the Pole to the equator by clocking the swing of a pendulum along a line between Dunkirk, France, and Barcelona, Spain. The meter was touted as a "natural" physical unit—one-ten-millionth of a quadrant of the Earth's great circle, or 1/40,000,000 of the circumference of the planet.

The metric system became law in France in 1799. You could

get a jail sentence for manufacturing or importing old-fashioned units of measure. Every county seat in the nation received its own registered copy of the original *Mètre Étalon*. Although women were not expected to understand the metric system, men and boys were encouraged to study it. The long-winded explanations published by the Academy of Sciences were written in a style reminiscent of today's computer manuals. Stumped by the intricacy of the new metric table of conversion establishing Greek prefixes for each multiple of ten (kilo-, hecto-, deca-, deci-, cent-, milli-) revolutionary craftsmen, merchants, and educators must have felt as frustrated as PC users trying to install the latest software upgrade in their outdated hardware system.

Adopted by 40 nations, the metric system was a commercial success. (Along with Burma and Liberia, the United States is the last country in the world that does not use the metric system on a regular basis, although an act signed in 1988 specified it as the preferred system.) In 1875, an international conference in Paris established the Sèvres museum, where the *Étalon* was ceremoniously placed in a special vault in its own little pavilion. In 1889, the international Treaty of the Meter was signed there. The authority of the standard went unchallenged until 1960, when the definition of the meter was reevaluated by modern instruments—and de-romanticized in the process. A meter is now the distance traveled by light in a vacuum in 1/299,792,458 seconds.

With an equally abstract mission, the measurement icon of the next generation may be the electronic measurer. A magic wand of sorts, it has been designed, like the original meter, to be a universal tool. Called the Ultrasonic Digital Measuring Meter, the $45 device, available at Brookstone, looks like a flashlight. It zaps distances, measuring them in feet and inches or metric units. All that is required is to aim at a target and squeeze; an integrated conversion calculator estimates the quantities of material needed for painting, carpeting, wallpapering, tiling, air-conditioning, and heating crunches the numbers for you.

But the digital meter's beam-me-up-Scotty approach reduces our complex spatial perceptions to a dull numeric experience. By removing the physical and intellectual involvement that measurements once required, it numbs both the mind and the senses. The meter standard, by contrast, connected people to the size of planet Earth, the number of fingers on their hands—and to an enlightened Gallic rationality. Someday, when we are all adrift in cyberspace, we will remember fondly the time when the basic unit of measure was a humble metal stick kept in a quaint museum located on the outskirts of the city of Paris.

Making a verbal commitment to machines
The first time my telephone asked me to answer questions by pressing keys or saying "yes," I was tempted to slam the receiver in its face. How dare the thing talk to me and expect a verbal commitment?

There was no way I was going to say "yes." Vanity kept me from talking into the mouthpiece to activate the device. Instead, I deliberately reached for the upper-left-hand corner of the keypad and pressed the first button, the number 1. There was a click and some inner mechanism dialed the number. "Now," I said to myself, "that's better."

That was the first time my telephone asked me to answer questions by either pressing keys or saying "yes," and I was tempted to slam the receiver in its face. How dare the thing talk to me and expect a verbal commitment? Machines aren't supposed to initiate dialogue with their users, or so I thought. Funny how class consciousness sneaks up on you. In retrospect, I suspect that I didn't want to interact with the electronic device for fear I'd be humiliated in front of the help. Servant-master prejudices die hard. Because they do menial tasks, we tend to treat machines like lackeys.

In Victorian households, servants were not educated. Culture was the prerogative of the upper class. In the nineteenth century, a laundress, a maid, or a scullion would have received severe punishment if she tried to learn to read and write. In that respect, we've come a long way. We now teach our machines all we know. We upgrade them constantly. We train them to think for themselves and take on managerial responsibilities. We even program them to sound like our favorite pop characters—some computers can quote Bugs Bunny, Captain Kirk, Bette Davis, or Arnold Schwarzenegger.

When George Eastman coined his famous slogan "You press the button, we do the rest," he unwittingly created a new social class of button barons. His one-dollar Brownie camera, introduced in 1900, put effortlessness within everybody's reach. Push-button devices, such as the cash register, the jukebox, the blender, and the car radio became great American icons, symbols of a new so-called classless society where appliances were the only flunkies. But this ideal world could disappear with a single hit of another, penultimate button: the nuclear button.

Capable of generating instant annihilation—or instant gratification—that flat ubiquitous knob was the twentieth century's arch villain as well as its unsung hero.

Like their push-button ancestors, first-generation electronic devices were designed to respond to gentle nudging. Some of their keys bob below the surface and then ricochet right back. Others resist all the way down, only to yield with a tactful click. My favorites are squeezably soft and feel like the plastic air bubbles you wrap stuff with. But as we enter the third millennium, it seems we must give up this hands-on approach—and take our fingers off the controls. Voice activation, a fast-growing technology perfected at last, is changing the way we operate machines. Just purse your lips and talk—the contraption will carry out your orders without your ever having to pull a switch, click a mouse, or press a button.

But for all their sophistication and learning abilities, computers are still lagging behind. Although there isn't much of a structural difference between the hardware and the wetware—between the anatomy of the $3,000 appliance sitting on my desk and the soggy mass floating in my skull—the conceptual capabilities of gray matter are far superior to that of chips. According to Paul Churchland, author of *The Engine of Reason, the Seat of the Soul,* human consciousness is the result of the firing of 100 billion neurons through their 100 trillion synaptic connections. Add to this the fact that the volume of each cell-to-cell connection is adjustable, and you've raised the power of the brain by $10^{100,000,000,000,000}$. To keep up with us, computers must slow us down. Paradoxically, the faster they get, the more impatient we become: good computers do a good job of slowing us down. To bridge the mental gap, programmers load their software with dialogue boxes that attempt to explain what the operating system is thinking about. But the limited vocabulary—OK, Cancel, Go, Search, Delete—only makes the communication more frustrating. What we call "interaction" is a systematic process of mental retardation.

Lengthy prerecorded phone messages ramble on, probably buying time while the circuits relay the digitalized information to the main processor. You wait for the tone; wait for the beep; wait for your cues to select the proper options; wait to leave your own rambling message. Willy-nilly, you learn to be more tolerant of these fastidious electronic office assistants. One of the most annoying interactive experiences is ordering movie tickets by phone. On average, you listen to about 30 different questions. You must answer six of them correctly to get your tickets. "Do you want to select your movie by name? Press 1. By theater? Press 2. By zip code? Press 3. By city? Press 4. By borough? Press 5. By content classification? Press 6." While you fight a case of nerves as you keep up with this rapid-fire interrogation, you can hear the electronic circuits humming leisurely.

Interactive systems have their own agenda. They tell you only what they want you to know. In New York, the Metropolitan Transit Authority (MTA) has been testing a modernistic rubber-and-steel subway train, a prototype that glides effortlessly on the old tracks. A soothing female voice welcomes you as soon as you step in, announcing the name of the next station and the approximate time of arrival. You can tell from the look on people's faces that it would take a lot more to impress New Yorkers. The lady is nice enough—but where's the beef? Is there a delay on the N and R lines connecting at 42nd Street? Is the local train far behind? Are there problem spots on the vast MTA network? When the next polite message comes in, wishing you a safe ride, people carefully avoid making eye contact, embarrassed by the patronizing tone of the computerized voice. A subway is a means of transportation—not a baby-sitting service.

Interactive devices do try to be helpful, but they are up against what we benignly call human nature—our innate ability to screw things up, learn from it, and move on. In an earnest attempt to make vertical transportation faster, an elevator company decided to eliminate the up and down buttons in hallways and replace them with a keypad. Instead of waiting for the next available car, riders punched in the floor number. A liquid display told them which elevator was assigned to them. You wouldn't have wanted to run to make it in before the doors closed, though. If you hadn't entered your destination into the computer, you'd have been trapped: There were no buttons inside the cars.

Voice activation, in its infancy, was actually an effective technique for holding people back. To communicate with machines, one had to enunciate carefully. The electronic protocol did not understand colloquialisms, snide remarks, or sloppy pronunciation. You couldn't bark at the hardware. You had to watch your manners. Polite conversation with a bunch of smart microchips was excruciatingly slow. The future of voice activation looked dim: In order to communicate with our software, we'd all have to learn to talk like Garrison Keillor.

Today, multiple-chip voice recognition allows computers to identify your voice, take dictation, and transcribe your speech—regardless of your accent. At home and in your car, security-minded chips are at your command, ready to turn on lights, open doors, or lower the blinds if you say so. A widely available phone feature lets you dial simply by saying into the mouthpiece the name of the person you want to reach. As unique as your fingerprints, your voice pattern is quickly becoming your universal access code.

Yet I still hesitate whenever I am given the option to punch keys or speak up to activate a phone function. For reasons I don't quite understand, I feel bashful when vocalizing in front of the circuitry. Recently, I decided to overcome my shyness once and for all. But as I took a deep breath, forming the word on my lips to release a resonant "yes," I saw myself standing at the altar, about to get married. Caught by surprise, mouth open, throat dry, I experienced a sudden flash of panic. I had an irrational urge to make a dash for the door. The same "I do" that joins two people in a life-long commitment is now required of us as we are wedded to our electronic future.

Alexander Liberman: on overcoming aesthetics
During his 50-plus-year career at Condé Nast,
editorial director Alexander Liberman
supervised magazines that were scripted to
have a dramatic plot line.

Alexander Liberman, the legendary editorial director of Condé Nast Publications (CNP), always insisted that magazines had to be readable. Readable? The magazines he supervised during his 50-plus-year career at CNP—*Vogue*, *Glamour*, *Self*, *House & Garden*, *Vanity Fair*, and others—had distinctively crowded, messy layouts: page after page incorporated jumbled montages of text and images. Forget about curling up quietly to read the articles; Liberman's signature look is much too lively to invite contemplation of that kind.

Liberman, who retired in 1994, never bothered reading a manuscript before laying out a story. Back when I was the art director of *Self* magazine, he once caught me reading a piece I was working on. With the authority of a man 30 years my senior, he reprimanded me severely for wasting time on the job. Magazine readers must get a feel for a story before reading it, he explained. It's best if art directors don't get involved with the text. My role, he said, was to communicate ideas—not illustrate words.

He summoned to my office the senior editor in charge. She scurried in, a hard copy of the edited manuscript pressed against her chest like a shield. She was asked to put it aside at once and pitch her story aloud to Liberman. Always polite and suave, Mr. Liberman, as we called him, rebuked her whenever she looked at her notes. He was not about to be text-driven. Whether dealing with fashion, beauty, health, food, or travel, articles in CNP magazines were scripted to have a dramatic plot line. With a series of questions, he tried to unveil the reader's emotional relationship with the article. "Are you saying that vitamins are bad for you?" he asked. "If that's so, rewrite the headline."

While listening to the editor, Liberman began to build a new layout from scratch, his hands moving as if on automatic pilot over the drawing board. "I don't search, I find," he liked to say, paraphrasing Picasso. Headlines, quotes, sidebars, photographs, dummy text, and pieces of colored paper would come together in less than three minutes. I had to hold my breath, literally, not to disturb this impromptu collage. As soon as Liberman declared that he was done, he made it clear that my responsibility was to hold the elements in place with tiny bits of transparent tape—and God help me if I straightened anything in the process.

David Carson, the now famous graphic design iconoclast whom I hired at *Self* in 1990 as a mere pasteup assistant, remembers trying to copy-fit Liberman's montages with the final text—not an easy task. "It was surreal," Carson now says. He had to treat Liberman's fragile piles of scrap paper as if they were works of art. He thought it was all pretty silly. "At the time I didn't know who this guy was. Now, looking back, I get the feeling that he has been undervalued and underappreciated as a graphic designer." Although the two never spoke, I can't help but wonder if Carson was not influenced by the old man's serendipitous approach to the page.

Though Liberman's layouts were at times deliberately messy, they were never confusing. He would strive to shock readers, but never intimidate them. As a result, the magazines he designed were approachable and thus "readable." He made sure that Condé Nast's publications triggered in readers an instant sense of identification with what was presented on the page. A glance is all one needed to grasp the sum total of what the editors were thinking about. These were magazines one didn't need to decipher in order to read. "Clarity and strength of communication is what interest me," said Liberman. "I hate white space because white space is an old album tradition. I need to be immersed in the subject matter."

Unfortunately, few of Liberman's collaborators were ever able to "read" him as effortlessly as readers were able to decipher his layouts. From 1942, when Liberman replaced the formidable Mehemed Fehmy Agha as art director of *Vogue* magazine, to 1994, when he announced that the young editor of *Details*, James Truman, would be his successor as CNP's editorial director, he kept everybody mystified with abrupt decisions and unexpected turnarounds. "The creative process is a series of destructions," he was fond of saying. For him, the creative process was also a series of dramatic dismissals. Great editors got the ax on Liberman's watch: Diana Vreeland, Grace Mirabella, Louis Oliver Gropp, to name just a few. And countless great art directors as well: Priscilla Peck, Lloyd Ziff, Derek Ungless, Ruth Ansel, Rip George.

Years after his death in 1998, the mere mention of Liberman can set off heated discussion among designers and editors who have worked with him. People who have been fired by him sometimes break out in hives. Others relish the opportunity to tell some particularly funny story. Because of him, there is an instant sense of community among ex-CNP employees. Commenting on Liberman's "absurdly hip" collage-approach, design critic Owen Edwards today says: "When I worked with him, I always thought he was dead wrong—which only shows how dead wrong I was."

Liberman had a knack for astounding and confusing people around him—and his attempts to explain his design philosophy were more alienating than reassuring. "Consistency is the sign of a small mind," he told me for openers. "Don't be stylish, you'll be dated," he would then admonish. And he kept after me: "*Un peu plus de brutalité, s'il vous plaît, ma chère amie*" (a little more brutality, please, my dear friend), he insisted when my fashion layouts looked too "nice" to him. And each time my heart would sink. But eager to please—no one was ever immune to his old-world charm—I presented the next day a revised, Fleet Street–inspired layout. Such a look of contempt I had never before endured. "Simply lurid," he said, before walking out of the room.

He was not a teacher. Although very articulate, he could never find the appropriate words to share his vision with others. Looking back, I believe that his inability to communicate with his design associates was due to the fact that his ideas were so radical, he couldn't begin to describe them. He used an anti-quated vocabulary that dated from the days of Gutenberg to introduce a way of thinking that foreshadowed the revolution of the information age. He asked for "vulgarity" when what he was after was impact. He talked of "charm" to describe a sense of ease. He called "provincial" layouts that were too rigid. Although Liberman dismissed computers as "too slow," ten years before the introduction of the Macintosh he was already designing pages as if they were interactive screens, with layered rather than linear narratives.

A man employees loved to describe as suave, urbane, and aristocratic, Liberman was no stranger to revolutions, cultural or otherwise. Born in Kiev, Russia, in 1912, he remembers the first days of the Bolshevik upheaval. His father, a powerful forestry and timber manager, prospered under Lenin's regime. His mother, an out-of-work actress, created a children's theater to keep starving urchins off the street. But in this climate of anarchy and social chaos, the young Liberman, a sensitive and difficult child, was displaying troubling behavioral symptoms. His parents were afraid he was turning into a delinquent. In 1921, apparently with Lenin's personal consent, he was shipped to school in England, where he was forced to learn manners. A quick study, he acquired there, by age 10, the genteel demeanor and slight British accent that would later become his trademark.

After Lenin's death in 1924, the Libermans left Russia and settled in Paris. Alex was transferred to a chic French private school, where he made valuable friends among the sons of the aristocracy. But the turning point for him was visiting the 1925 Paris *Arts Décoratifs* exhibition. He was only a teenager, yet the discovery of Art Deco, then called Art Moderne, was "one of the most important events in my life," he said later.

From then on, the concept of modernity became something of an obsession with him: "Alex tried and tried to get everyone to be modern—his idea of modern," notes Lloyd Ziff, who was the art director at *House & Garden*, *Vanity Fair*, and *Traveler* in the 1980s. He also points out that the way Liberman worked, juxtaposing photographic and typographical elements, was more reminiscent of Russian Constructivism than of French Art Deco.

Liberman's early career in design was somewhat erratic. A bleeding ulcer kept interrupting his attempts to find a line of work he would enjoy. He studied painting with André Lhote, architecture with Auguste Perret, and was briefly employed by Cassandre. In 1933, he got a job at *VU*, a Parisian weekly and one of the very first news magazines to use reportage photography. There, he befriended Lucien Vogel, the editor, and met photographers who would help him define his taste for photojournalism: André Kertész, Robert Capa, and Brassaï.

In the late 1930s, after a brief marriage to Hilda Sturm, a German ski champion, Liberman fell deeply in love with a married woman, Tatiana du Plessis. She was a striking beauty and a niece of the famous Russian actor and director Konstantin Stanislasky, inventor of method acting. The invasion of France by Hitler's army in 1940 forced their fate: Tatiana's aristocratic French husband was killed while trying to join exiled general Charles de Gaulle in England. Alex escaped to New York with Tatiana, soon to be his wife, and her daughter, Francine.

In New York, Liberman was quickly hired by Condé Nast. Founder of the company that still bears his name, Nast was impressed with Liberman's experience with photojournalism at *VU*. Back in 1931, Clare Booth Luce had submitted to Nast, her boss at the time, the prototype for a weekly picture magazine called *Life*. He had rejected it. Now *Life*, launched in the late thirties by Henry Luce, Clare's husband, was a success—and Nast was sorry he had missed the opportunity to start a breakthrough publication. When Liberman proposed during his job interview to inject some reportage into *Vogue*, Nast loved it. From that day on, Alex Liberman thought of himself as a journalist—a super editor with visual understanding. He never liked the title of art director and was relieved when, in 1962, he was appointed editorial director of all Condé Nast magazines.

During his career at CNP, Liberman actually carried a grudge against art directors. Their title, he felt, was misleading. He didn't want them to be artists, but managers of the image of the magazine. He understood his role, and the role of all editorial designers, to be what we call today "brand managers." Unfortunately, the notion of branding was still in its infancy, and Liberman never came across the use of that term. What a pity. He would have loved to wrestle with concepts such as "perceived quality," "brand equity," and "visual territory."

Instead of rewriting the art director's job description, Liberman spent five decades fighting the idea that editorial design was an artistic endeavor. He went out of his way to undermine art directors in front of editors. With remarks like "This layout is utterly banal, wouldn't you say?," or "Remember: You are not a scarf designer, you are a journalist," he could reduce some of the most talented designers to tears. In the hallways of CNP, you could easily spot art directors: they were the walking wounded—the folks wearing neck braces. While at *Self*, I too became partially disabled with a frozen shoulder, tension migraines, and lower back problems.

Editors who attended the daily public floggings of art directors would look at their shoes in embarrassment—but internally, they were rubbing their hands. Liberman can be credited with weakening the authority of editorial art directors in the U.S. He trained three generations of editors to belittle the opinion of their visually oriented coworkers. Today, every publication in America has at least one editor who once worked at CNP and refers to Quark Xpress and Photoshop users as "my art people."

Liberman considered art direction a profession, not an "art." As far as he was concerned, art was something one did in a studio, not in an office. In fact, in his spare time, during weekends, he managed to become a prolific artist—furiously painting huge canvases or making large-scale environmental sculptures that won critical acclaim in the New York art world. As such,

Liberman led two distinct lives. Careful to cultivate a Clark Kent, charcoal-gray-suit persona by day, he would become an ambitious Abstract Expressionist by night. His wife, Tatiana, called him Superman. "Art is the violent expression of resentment against the human condition," he told Barbara Rose, the author of a monograph on his work as an artist. Rose was under the impression that Liberman kept that resentment a private matter. "Alexander Liberman, the artist, is deeply suspicious of taste," she wrote in 1981. "Alexander Liberman, the editorial director of CNP, is, above all, a man of taste."

Rose was misinformed. With each passing year at CNP, Liberman showed less and less patience with issues of taste, letting his growing resentment show through. He became committed to banishing forever the "vision of loveliness" he had endured at the beginning of his tenure at Condé Nast from the very proper ladies who were *Vogue*'s early editors: Josephine Redding, Marie Harrison, Edna Woolman Chase, and Jessica Daves. At long last, in the 1960s, Diana Vreeland set him free. "Laying out a beautiful picture in a beautiful way is a bloody bore," she once said. Like him, she treated the magazine as a series of collages, wantonly pasting together her models' body parts to get the "perfect whole." Liberman was impressed. "I put legs and arms and heads together," she said. "I never took out fewer than two ribs."

When I first encountered Liberman, in the late 1970s, Diana Vreeland had been replaced by Grace Mirabella, and the *Vogue* art department, where I worked as a pasteup assistant, was run by Rochelle Udell. The magazine layouts were deliberately untidy, to differentiate *Vogue* from its competition, *Harper's Bazaar*, the absolute leader in terms of design and visual innovation. Still under the influence of its legendary art director Alexey Brodovitch, *Bazaar* was a thorn in Liberman's side. But he did what a good brand manager would do: instead of trying to play catch-up with *Bazaar*, he carved out a new, younger niche for *Vogue*. As soon as he did that, circulation began to rise dramatically. And advertisers loved being associated with a smart fashion publication that embraced the spirit of the Pepsi generation.

As David Carson would do 15 years later, I spent long hours in the *Vogue* art department, painstakingly trying to fit type around Liberman's complex photomontages. Meanwhile, in his studio at home, the "Silver Fox," as some editors now called him, was throwing paint by the bucketful on oversized canvases, working as fast as possible to try to bypass the mental process that he believed could produce only preconceived and banal solutions.

In 1989, I jumped at the opportunity to work with him again, this time at *Self*. By now, Liberman had dropped all pretense of good taste. Although he had retained his suave, David Niven look, I was told that he was fiercer than ever. And indeed, Anthea Disney, the editor who had hired me, was fired soon after I joined CNP for not following Liberman's directions. In no position to assert myself with the new editor, Alexandra Penney, I decided to look at the situation as a chance to resolve the Liberman mystery once and for all. I galvanized my staff and made it clear to Liberman that my entire art department was at his service. For the next six months, we were on a roll.

As soon as the great man walked into the room, we were ready in battle formation: One assistant was at my side with scissors, knife, and loupe; another was posted next to the color copier; a third was assigned to the phones to keep the lines open in case Liberman got a call. I had two "runners" ready to fetch an editor, find a color swatch, or alert the photo department. Helen Maryles, the youngest designer, was on tape duty. I will never forget the sight of her, standing next to Liberman, palms open, fingers extended, with tiny pieces of transparent tape stuck at the end of her ten digits.

In his biography, *Alex*, written by Dodie Kazanjian and Calvin Tomkins, Liberman says: "If ever I have done what I'd call my own layouts, it's at *Self*." The pages he designed there were a debauch of bold type and cut-paper blocks of colors, a look reminiscent of the *papiers découpés* technique Matisse favored at the end of his career. Liberman had met him briefly in 1949, when the painter was in his late seventies—still alert and youthful in spite of age and poor health. Now, Liberman had a chance to emulate his favorite artist. The *Self* layouts were an unmitigated homage to the author of *The Dance*.

For the first time ever, Liberman was doing "art" at the office. He did concede to his biographers that at *Self* there was "not much difference in the psychological process between a composition on canvas and arranging material like this on a page." So this was it. In a long career dedicated to overcoming aesthetic considerations, the *Self* experiment represented a brief moment of reconciliation between the editorial director and the artist—between Clark Kent and Superman.

The vehicle of this reconciliation was a commercial disaster. The advertisers hated the "new" *Self*, with its whimsical color-blocks and elegant yet topsy-turvy typography. The readers didn't get it either. The newsstand circulation took a nose dive. The magazine had lost its sacrosant "readability." Liberman, in collaboration with me and my staff, had been breaking his own rules—having fun and doing "art" at the office instead of striving to keep the layouts upbeat and accessible. I was fired—and rightly so—for encouraging a 78-year-old man to be creative on the job.

A uniquely American concept
Branding a product and marketing
its brand above and beyond the product
itself is a uniquely American concept—
one that isn't popular on the other
side of the Atlantic. In Europe,
Coke is just a beverage.

These days, most Europeans look at American culture with a mixture of awe and anguish. The increasing ubiquity of American brand names in their lives makes them leery. My twenty-something French niece, for instance, works on an iMac, subscribes to America Online, watches CNN, uses a Visa card, buys Calvin Klein fragrances, wears Gap jeans, and thinks it's cool to meet friends for ice cream at the Häagen-Dazs café on the Champs Elysées. She gets annoyed, though, when I point out to her that these brands, which help define her self-image, are in fact American creations. For her, U.S. brands are the medium, not the message.

I noticed that it's usually the European kids with the Levi's jeans, the Ralph Lauren T-shirts, and the Nike sneakers who are the most anxious about this new form of cultural colonization. They sure love American products, but they distrust the tidings that come with them. When asked what it is exactly they like or dislike about it, they make a face, bite their lips, cross their arms on their chest, and look down at their shoes. They won't tell. It's something way beyond your average love-hate relationship—it's more like a fatal attraction.

American culture has always made Europeans nervous, but these days, with the unification of Europe a complex reality, there is a different quality to their trepidation. For Europe, America is both a role model and a warning. It's the thing you want to emulate—and it's the thing you want to avoid.

My niece does not object to the quality or the design of the American goods she buys. In fact, she loves them. We've come a long way since the days of the Ugly American. The aesthetic values of most of the products and advertising campaigns from U.S. companies are just as sophisticated and just as smart as anything that comes out of Italy, Germany, or France. What annoys my niece about American products versus, let's say, German products, is their emotional context. The American stuff is more than simply stuff—it's a concept, it's an attitude, it's a value system. In other words, it's a brand.

Branding a product and marketing its brand above and beyond the product itself is a uniquely American concept—one that isn't popular on the other side of the Atlantic. Heirs to Francis Bacon, Copernicus, Galileo, and Descartes, Europeans believe that selling images is something on the order of idol-worship—a practice for heathens, savages, and fetishists. Three hundred years of Rationalism have taught them to celebrate reason, not emotions. To them, Coke is a beverage. The subliminal message compressed into the visual symbolism of the ubiquitous red swirl on the can makes no impression on them. Or at least that's what they would like to think.

So it comes as no surprise that European brands are a lot more demure than American ones. But so what? We still have Paris, right? Well, maybe not. As multinationals are taking control of the playing field, even the City of Lights is starting to look like an American suburban mall. Local brands cannot protect their territory against the likes of IBM, Philip Morris, Procter & Gamble, Colgate Palmolive, Paramount Pictures, Mattel, or Disney—or even against smaller American image merchants like Ralph Lauren, the Gap, or Donna Karan, relative newcomers to the Euro scene. There are a few notable exceptions, such as Lancôme, Chanel, and Louis Vuitton, which have developed American-style branding strategies in order to compete in the States among U.S. rivals like Estée Lauder or Revlon.

Who would've guessed that as the dust settled on the American century, marketing—not literature, Pop Art, movies, music, or even television—would emerge as the defining medium for the remaining superpower. Today, the real American folk heroes (or villains, depending how you see them) are not the John Waynes, James Deans, or the Liz Taylors of the silver screen, but the Clinique ads, the iMac commercials, the Absolut campaigns, and the Barbie Dolls wearing Calvin Klein outfits—even the gaunt Calvin Klein models themselves. As far as the world at large is concerned, that's what this country is all about.

Not people, but logos. Not principles, but trademarks. Not democracy—brands.

But too many brands, too little time. The one thing Americans understand better than anyone else on this planet is how to create desires for things no one needs or even has time to use. They make it almost impossible for folks to be satisfied with what they already have. They don't simply ignore other people's culture and traditions—they make the very concept of history obsolete.

To distance yourself from your past, develop brand awareness. The Cambodian priest who sips from a can of Pepsi, the Chinese boy wearing a Joe Camel sweatshirt, and the Iranian youth with the Converse sneakers are deliberately trying to break away from their traditions. The right logo embossed, silkscreened, or stitched on a piece of goods becomes the official stamp on a new passport that gives them permission to put their identity as consumers before their national pride.

The increasing pervasiveness of American brands in Europe is probably a sign that future members of the European Economic Community (the EEC) are ready to let go of their most jingoistic instincts in order to come together as one united tribe. In his 1973 book *The Americans: The Democratic Experience*, author Daniel Boorstin tells how, 200 years ago in America, the development of commercial trademarks helped create a coherent culture. Back then, brands gave immigrants who had nothing in common a shared medium. He notes that brand names "drew together in novel ways people who might not otherwise have been drawn together at all.... The particular importance of American consumption communities made it easier to assimilate, to 'Americanize' the millions who arrived here since the Civil War."

The branding phenomenon sweeping Europe today is not unlike the phenomenon that helped create a sense of commonwealth among American pioneers. There is one important difference though: The new Europeans are more likely to rally around an American brand than around one of their many local favorites. It's a lot easier for people of different backgrounds to love—or hate—Big Macs than to combine the subtle flavor of French Papillon blue cheese with a sip of Italian Barolo red wine.

Unlike European brands that demand prior understanding of the local cultural mores to be appreciated, American brands are simple narratives based on universal emotions. Take Joe Camel, for example. Where did he get that insolent and haughty temperament that appeals to smokers with a rebellious mindset? It was purely accidental. The original logo was drawn from a photograph of a Barnum & Bailey dromedary taken when the circus happened to pass through Winston-Salem in 1913. During the photo shoot, "Old Joe," as the beast was called, wouldn't keep still, so his trainer hit him on the nose—thus the outraged look and the raised tail of the one-humped mammal on the package. The genius of the marketing team at R.J. Reynolds Tobacco was to exploit this incident, turn it into a major component of their brand, and develop a consistent stream of imagery to support it.

The powerful supermarket brands of today all have humble and accessible origins as well. They were created by people who needed easy solutions to everyday problems. Band-Aid came about when the young wife of a Johnson & Johnson employee kept burning her fingers on her kitchen stove. Her husband sat down one night and devised a bandage even a klutz could apply. The Gerber baby was born in Fremont, Michigan, in 1928, a couple of months after Dan Gerber's own baby was switched to solid food. And legend has it that Wade Morrison, a young pharmacist from Virginia, named his soft drink creation Dr. Pepper after his fiancée's dad, in a vain attempt to win the old man's approval.

The most serendipitous of all brand narratives is probably Ivory Soap. In fact, it was a gift from heaven. Harley Procter, of Procter and Gamble fame, was sitting in church listening to the minister's sermon one Sunday in 1878, trying to come up with a name for his new white soap, the one that's "so pure, it floats," when he heard the preacher's words: "Out of the ivory palaces...whereby they have made thee glad." America's most popular soap got its name from Psalm 45:8.

Aware of the powerful impact of anecdotes, American marketers today create fantasy narratives for their brands, deliberately incorporating odd, trumped-up biographical or historical details into the symbolism and iconography of their visual vocabulary. Their methodology combines an intuitive approach with daring faux rationalization—in ways that would make Descartes and other enlightened philosophers and historians turn in their graves. Leslie Wexner, the visionary Columbus, Ohio, merchant who put Victoria's Secret, Abercrombie & Fitch, and Express on the directory of every mall in America, pushes the envelope even further by asking his brand managers to make up names and biographies for the imaginary wife, children, and pets of the fictitious founders of his various retail chains.

The ambivalence of European consumers toward marketing in general and brands in particular is directly proportionate to their high concept of historical accuracy. One of the biggest brand success stories in Europe is probably Chanel, a fashion empire based on a minor historical character who has been cleverly marketed into a legend.

So maybe it's time we drop our *Encyclopedia Britannica* approach to culture and adopt a deliberately revisionist view of history. For more and more people, traditional analysis of data does not tell the whole story any longer. Recently, a friend of mine mentioned that he was flying down to Miami on PanAm. "You aren't flying on PanAm," I said sanctimoniously, "you are flying in an airplane with the old PanAm logo painted on its tail. Don't be fooled: a small airline bought the right to use the logo of the once famous airline." I felt smug, but the look of chagrin on his face made me wish I had kept my mouth shut. In our day and age, you don't belittle someone's brand. It's like denigrating his or her fundamental values. For him, flying PanAm was a profound reality that had nothing to do with my linear view of the facts.

Today, brands are treated by branding experts as purely emotional concepts, endowed with a private life of their own and operating almost independently from the products they incarnate. In fact, while the goods and services the best brands represent are perceived as reliable, the brands themselves are designed to appear vulnerable—with subtle character flaws that make their personality more believable. Nike is somewhat ruthless. Gucci struts its stuff, aloof and arrogant. Victoria's Secret is deliciously naughty. Martha Stewart makes no attempt to curb her controlling impulses. Imperfect like people, yet strangely likeable for their human frailty, these brands elicit in consumers the same admiration as movie stars, sports heroes, or talk show hosts. They are celebrities, glamorous yet not beyond our reach.

But make no mistake: Although the best brands affect a lifelike vulnerability in order to be more accessible, the products they personify cannot disappoint customers. When you ask French people why they still patronize McDonald's, they praise the cleanliness of the "McDo" restaurants, the speed of service, the affordable prices—and the taste of the Big Macs. The *taste* of the Big Macs? In the land of steak au poivre and boeuf bourguignon? You bet. In the mind of the customers, there is more to a brand than its sizzle. To justify our choices, we invoke perceived qualities—and for brand managers worldwide, these subjective endorsements are money in the bank.

Object lesson #1: the chair
As far as I am concerned, when you sit
in a chair, people are likely to fire you,
reprimand you, or even worse, lecture you.

"**C**lose the door and sit down," she said, pointing at a chair. I sat down and felt dizzy, as if I was experiencing a tremendous loss of altitude. Only 12 inches separated my standing from my sitting position, yet it felt like a long way down. "I am sorry," said my boss. "We have to let you go."

I never liked being asked to sit down. "Sit down" always means bad news in my experience. While an empty chair suggests that you are expecting company, the same chair can feel like a restraining device when you are asked to sit in it. As far as I am concerned, when you sit in a chair, people are likely to fire you, reprimand you, or even worse, lecture you.

I come from a line of people who never sat down. My paternal grandfather, a typesetter, spent his life standing in front of a workbench, laying out pages of copy by hand, line after line, one letter at a time. Far from being a sedentary activity, metal typesetting was done on one's feet, requiring in the early days a tremendous mental and physical involvement. Each carved letter had to be handled separately, sorted out and then bundled together with each other to form words in an endless and graceful spelling ballet. As a result, I have always admired professionals who work standing up—maîtres d'hôtel, stand-up comics, teachers. They seem freer, less strained than those whose work requires them to sit down. Upright, alert, and in movement, you feel like a kite leaning against the wind.

A free spirit, my grandfather did not want to be tied down. By the time his third child was born, it must've gotten to him. My grandmother told me how he came into the bedroom to see my father, his newborn son, but could not bring himself to look at the baby. "He took off his hat, put it on a chair, and, in his confusion, sat on it," she remembered. "He remained motionless and speechless, utterly uncomfortable. After a while he stood up, left the room, and never came back." She was left with three kids, and the memory of the chair with his crumpled hat.

I inherited his fascination for typography and his mixed feelings toward chairs. I became an art director and, constantly on the move to meet various deadlines, I seldom sat down. Soon I realized that the printed page and the chair have a common ambition—they both compete for authority.

Early in my career, I worked for a newspaper editor who was famous for his paternalistic managerial style and for the pair of antique barber chairs he kept in his office. He believed in the all-mighty authority of the printed word—and in the power of his executive throne. Whenever he met potential contributors, he would sit them down in one of his monumental chairs as if they were about to get their first haircut, while he sat across the desk in his own high-back swivel-tilt leather armchair. He would invariably start his interview with the same standard question: "What do you want to be when you grow up?" It was a silly routine, but no one ever thought it was funny. There is something humiliating—almost unbearably so—about being questioned while sitting in a barber's chair.

Eventually he was pushed into retirement and sent home with his barber chairs. A woman half his age replaced him. She liked to conduct editorial meetings perched on the edge of what used to be his desk. Swinging her feet back and forth like a little girl, she would giggle and look like she was about to get her first haircut. You almost wished she'd grow up. You almost wished she'd sit in an executive throne.

A chair is nothing more than the imprint of an attitude. It's the mold into which we pour our mental posture. Traditional men, for instance, manage to gain stature when they sit down. They command attention by simply lowering their center of gravity. The seat of their power is below the belt—they feel mighty good when they sit on their tail.

That's why I would like to take down all the statues of Rodin's *Thinker*—these humorless bronze castings portraying a naked man, sitting on a rock, deep in thought. We brought down the statues of Lenin; why not finish the job and get rid of this other symbol of oppressive superiority? Cultural clichés, the sculptures can be found in front of libraries, theaters, and museums the world over. Since the first unveiling of *The Thinker* in Paris in 1906, more people have been intimidated into believing that sitting with a stern look on one's face is a sign of intelligence and creativity.

A world without *The Thinker* would be a different world; this new world may be a place where people think on their feet, get on with it, and move ahead. It may be a world without armchairs, an intriguing yet not inconceivable thought. There are some early warning signs. In open-plan, Internet start-up companies coast to coast, big executive chairs are losing their status. The casual dress code and the flat hierarchy encourages higher-ups to voluntarily forgo their overassertive seat of power. Everyone, from the receptionist to the company founder, wants to sit in an Aeron chair, a pricey webbed contraption that looks like a tennis racket and encourages people to move, tilt, recline, and bounce around.

Interaction is replacing authority. As managerial types are forced on their feet, they must develop the stamina of an athlete to keep up with their busy 24/7 schedule. In meetings they stand up and run the show. In hallways, they hurry to their next meeting, a cell phone glued to their ear; at their workstation, they pace back and forth while teleconferencing with colleagues making a connection at O'Hare on their way to Singapore. Who wants an imperial-looking seat when sitting is the last thing you do—usually around 9 PM, when at long last no one is around to bug you and you get a chance to catch up with the day?

Chairs are losing some of their rigid heraldic appeal, but they are also losing their ability to evoke comfort and ease. Most of us are too busy to take the time to sit, like our parents did, in big easy chairs. We read our mail standing up, we recline in bed while eating dinner. How often do we sit around the dining room table for a formal meal? Sometimes we pull up a chair—only to lean on it while removing our clothes.

Are comfortable chairs becoming redundant? Were they necessary but temporary implements, soon to be replaced by more sophisticated devices? Are we saving our old-fashioned chairs only as anthropological evidence?

Although we will probably always sit down, the reasons for sitting will keep changing. Chairs, for instance, didn't have to be comfortable in the old days. One of the roots of the word chair is *cathedra*. It seems that in the beginning a chair was an architectural construction, not a piece of furniture. It was built to designate the place where power dwelt. It looked like a shelter, a sanctuary, or a shrine. Sometimes portable, chairs were meant nonetheless to establish a sense of permanence. They were heavy, with solid back and side panels and even canopies. In ancient Egypt, Greece, and Rome, chairs were thrones reserved for pharaohs, emperors, high magistrates, noblemen. There is no indication that sitting down in a primitive wooden throne was supposed to be particularly enjoyable—it was part of a job. To be isolated in one of those rigid enclosures during a religious ceremony or a state affair must have been like donning a bulky ritualistic vestment or a cumbersome military costume.

People did not sit in chairs to be comfortable but to be empowered. The ruling class chose to sit down to create a sense of stability, dependability, and perseverance. In contrast, the intellectual elite chose to stand to express their spiritual alertness. Priests officiated standing up. They knelt in prayer, but preached the Gospel on their feet. The great philosophers of antiquity believed that pacing around was the best way to stimulate mental activity. They compared reasoning to a voyage, a step-by-step process. Plato founded a school that was named the Academy, after a nearby garden where he and his students would meet to stroll and discuss philosophical topics. Aristotle, his star disciple, developed the peripatetic approach, a method of teaching based on walking back and forth while reasoning. In the Middle Ages, monks did most of their meditating in cloisters, walking round secluded peristyles, punctuating their thoughts with the sound of their footsteps on the polished stone pavement.

In the early days of Christianity, reading, like thinking, was a rhythmical activity. The few who could read stood at the lectern in front of an audience and read aloud. Reading quietly is a truly modern concept, one that implies the idea of privacy. Although monks knew solitude and isolation, they did not know privacy. Privacy means specialness, separateness, and a sense of individuality.

When children learn to read, they first read aloud. Remember the first time you experienced a book as an inner journey—and how it gave you a tremendous sense of individuality? St. Anselme, archbishop of Canterbury at the turn of the last millennium, was the first man we know of who read silently to himself, an eccentricity that heralded a change in the way we think about thinking. But the concept was slow to mature. It would take another 400 years for Gutenberg to invent printing—and for the widely available written word to make personal thoughts a more tangible and accessible reality for many.

As soon as people had books they wanted chairs, because chairs, unlike benches or even stools, are enclosed spaces that grant you a degree of privacy. From then on, one sat in a chair to be left alone. Rodin's *Thinker* wishes he could be left alone. He is trying to block out the outside world. Given a chair, he would look less worried and feel less frustrated and not quite so…naked.

For most of us, the ideal chair is a protective cocoon, a capsule in which to curl up around a favorite daydream—or around a favorite book. The ideal chair is probably your mother's womb. Reluctantly, we all agree that chairs should be functional, but we are not sure how to define function. Ergonomic studies of the body in action have contributed to the design of chairs that claim to "adjust to our physical environment." But even if they bounce up and down, tilt and roll, and let you fidget and stretch, make no mistake—chairs are not sneakers. They are designed to keep you in a seated position, concentrated on your work, allowing just enough movement to keep your blood circulating and your mind alert on the task at hand. You sit down in a chair not to adjust to, but on the contrary to block out specific aspects of the physical environment.

Intellectual efforts and vague reveries have one thing in common: They are forms of escape. Sit in a chair, in a focused or foggy frame of mind, and in both cases you will expect to distance yourself from physical reality. The role of a chair—any chair—is to neutralize the body. A chair is a sophisticated paralyzing device. As soon as you settle down, it goes to work. Your body puts up a small fight; it twists around hoping to make some adjustments; it leans forward to release the pressure points on the spine; it stretches the legs to lessen the strain developing in the thighs; if your body had any sense, it would get up and run. But that's just it—it has been desensitized. Designed to hamper your movements in order to free your mind, a chair is in fact a body trap. That's why we are physically attracted to chairs the way small insects are attracted to poisonous flowers. Like petals turned expectantly toward the light, the seat, the armrests, and the back panel are enticing us with the promise of a delicious embrace. Fragile and elegant on their stem-like legs, chairs look innocent enough. But beware...ornate, colorful, intriguing, they are predators quietly waiting for you to come within their range.

I should rejoice—the era of Rodin's *Thinker* is probably over. The way we think about thinking is changing one more time. New imperatives, new directions, and new concerns are shaping the way we do everything, from eating to working to resting. The electronic hive is the new metaphor. As thinking itself becomes a less private and personal endeavor, sitting is developing into an integrated process involving more people and more physical activity. The latest handheld computers are becoming genuine extensions of the self and are fusing with the body. Wearable PCs that hang from your shoulder, your belt, your wrist, your neck, your head, are coming off the drawing board. Soon, most of us will own those portable computer systems with earphones and tiny screens attached to headgear that deliver images that seem to float in space. Like Plato, we will be able to study and assess the situation as we go. There will be no need to sit down to think it over.

The end of an era is often marked by a great outburst of creativity. There is today an unprecedented profusion of extraordinary sitting objects. Chairs you can hardly sit on because they are too small, too deep, or too low. Chairs that look like they came out of the trash. Chairs so ornate, you'd like to wear them as costume jewelry. Chairs as hard as washboards. Chairs as fragile as ballroom gowns. Chairs shaped like question marks. There is a lack of restraint and a sense of dissipation. The Chair is dead. Long live The Chair.

Maintaining a consistent level of creativity Push Pin shattered the conservative design ethos of the 1950s. To contend with photography, illustrators had to offer something more. The members of the Push Pin consortium were the first to figure out what that "something" was.

I n the 1950s, no one aspired to be young. On the contrary, baby-faced adolescents wore traditional blazers, white shirts, and ties in order to look more grown-up. Artists and creative types, always suspected of being immature, sported expensive tweed jackets and smoked pipes in an attempt to cut an authoritative figure. Even rebels were older people. In 1955, Salvador Dalí was 51, Buckminster Fuller was 60, Le Corbusier was 68, and Picasso was 78. Emblematic of the period was President Dwight Eisenhower, a man in his mid-60s.

It was in this conservative climate that the Push Pin "style" came into existence—ten years before the youth phenomenon it eventually helped define. The Push Pin group burst onto the scene as a virtual entity at first. Before the studio was officially incorporated, the members of the Push Pin group were already known to graphic cognoscenti for their clever self-promotion—a witty publication called *The Push Pin Almanack*. A compilation of "the choicest morsels of essential information gathered for those persons in the graphic arts," it was mailed to 1,500 art directors on a bimonthly basis. It generated enough phone calls and assignments to keep its authors, all of them Cooper Union art students, from taking dead-end jobs in art studios.

A few issues of these small pamphlets have been preserved, their yellowing pages as fragile as the wings of some extinct lepidopteran. These diminutive, 3³/₄" x 8¹/₄" booklets show a singular editorial vigor. Illustrated by then-unknown artists—Edward Sorel, Seymour Chwast, Milton Glaser, Reynold Ruffins—their content is an odd compilation of serendipitous material in the style of the old American farmers' almanacs. Quotes by Machiavelli fraternize with advice on how to clean carpets. Whimsical woodcuts consort with audacious typographical exercises. The rudimentary, two-color process is systematically exploited to create maximum brilliance.

Back then, illustrators would advertise their work by sending art directors printed blotters. Printed blotters? "In the days of pen and ink, when people still wrote letters with fountain pens, blotters were popular," explains Ed Sorel. "But with the advent of the ballpoint pen, promotional blotters became obsolete. We had to come up with a novel way to let advertising agencies know that we were around." Soon, people came to associate the unorthodox orange-and-pink or navy-and-green color combinations of the *Almanack* with the name of the group. Push Pin was a style even before it was a studio. Ed's former wife, Elaine Sorel, remembers that the style of the *Almanack* was so fresh, it had imitators right away. "In hindsight, I now realize that part of the fascination with that look was the fact that it heralded the end of the Modernist rule," she says.

In the early 1950s, the world of illustration was due for a change. American illustrators were working in the narrative genre on large canvases that had to be shipped to magazines or advertising agencies at great expense. To the chagrin of these wannabe Rembrandts, major improvements in the quality of color photography (better paper, more sensitive film, faster processing and cheaper reproduction techniques) were enabling photographers to deliver realistic images at a price that was competitive with color illustrations. To contend with photography, illustrators had to offer something more. The members of the Push Pin consortium were the first to figure out what that "something" was. Instead of painting bigger, brighter, and bolder illustrations, they set out to develop conceptual images.

Conceptual illustration was not a new idea in Europe, where Italian graphic designer Armando Testa and Polish artist Tadeusz Trekowski were borrowing from the Surrealist vocabulary to create startling posters. But their innovative approach was ignored in the U.S. until, ironically, photography forced illustrators to rethink their craft. Free at long last from the iconographic responsibilities of linear storytelling (a job photographers were now doing), a new generation of pictorialists was interpreting rather than illustrating ideas. "We were working on paper, not canvas," recalls James McMullan, now famous for his Lincoln Center Theater posters, who joined Push Pin in the mid-sixties. "Integrating words with images, as we did in our conceptual illustrations, was perceived as a European thing. But to overcome the limitations of the printing process, we began to think about the whole page."

In an interview with Peter Mayer in 1972, Milton Glaser explains how his decision to become a conceptual designer/illustrator was an expression of his love of calligraphy and typography—but it also stemmed from a desire to gain control. "I [stayed] away from situations in which I would have to entrust my illustration to someone's else notion of design," he said. Now—more than a quarter of a century later—he comments: "Somehow, I was always good at putting information together in a way people could understand."

Being able to put words and images together was a valuable skill in the mid-1950s. It was the dawn of the information age. While television sets were invading living rooms, print media were experiencing tremendous growth and quality paperbacks were making culture much more accessible. "We had come to the end of the evolution of the Modernist style," explains Seymour Chwast. "We began to look around for new sources of inspiration. It was a timely process of discovery. We started investigating art from the beginning of the century and moved chronologically up, from Victoriana to Art Nouveau, and then to what, in my innocence, I called the 'Roxy' style. I only realized later that it was Art Deco."

Although the Push Pin illustrators admired their mentors—Ben Shahn, Cassandre, Bradbury Thompson, Paul Rand—they felt no pressure to follow in their footsteps. "We were ready to turn a corner," says Paul Davis, who became a member of the Push Pin Studios in the late 1950s. "We weren't compelled to be minimalist or modern. We invented postmodernism before it was even a concept."

In retrospect, it's easy to see where it all began—with the unassuming *Push Pin Almanack*. No heavier than a pack of seeds, it contained all the principles that, eventually, nurtured a fertile new crop of talented, eclectic, individualistic graphic designers. There could have been no better metaphor for this seminal publication than, indeed, a farmers' almanac.

In August 1954, Milton Glaser, who had been away in Italy on a Fulbright scholarship to study etching under Giorgio Morandi, came back to New York, and the Push Pin Studio was formed. "In those low-tech days, it took very little cash to go into business," recalls Chwast. "At the beginning, we didn't have a grand plan. We just needed a space to do our freelance work. We certainly had no idea Push Pin was going to be as influential as it was." Sorel, Ruffins, Chwast, and Glaser rented a flat in a small brownstone on East 17th Street, in what was the first of a series of temporary spaces that would house them for the next decade. "We were so determined to minimize our expenses that we only had a pay phone in the studio," says Sorel. "We had to drop a dime for each call." It was only in 1965 that Chwast and Glaser gathered enough capital to buy a building at 207 East 32 Street—an elegant limestone town house now considered a landmark in the history of graphic design in America—and the place where Milton Glaser still has his studio.

Back in 1954, the four partners had briefly toyed with the idea of changing the Push Pin name, deemed too frivolous by that period's standards, for something more serious, more adult. But they soon realized that it was too late to pry the catchy little words from their peers' consciousness. Like a thumbtack, it had stuck. And so had the *Almanack*. In addition to the growing mailing list of art directors in the New York area, the young illustrators were now getting requests for their in-house newsletter from readers from Los Angeles to East Berlin. Recast as *The Push Pin Monthly Graphic*, the original *Almanack* became a more sophisticated promo piece. First, it was published as a series of poster-size broadsheets; later it adopted a tabloid format. "While it seldom managed to live up to the 'monthly' part of its name," says Myrna Davis, who edited the publication from 1960 to 1965, "it certainly fulfilled its 'graphic' promise."

For the founders of Push Pin, the most important promise was to themselves. They all defined success as being able to maintain a consistent level of creativity. "We never confused the meaning of the work with how we were rewarded for it," says Milton Glaser. Right from its inception, the studio was organized to encourage its members to channel their energy creatively. "The place was structured in an unstructured way," says Phyllis Rich Flood, who was hired in 1969 to mastermind Push Pin's public relations. "There was no hierarchy—yet everyone had a real sense of productivity and responsibility to deadlines." It was all very efficient. According to Barry Zaid, a Canadian illustrator who worked at Push Pin in the early 1970s, "there was always someone to pick up the pieces behind you so that you could do your best work at all times." Ruffins credits Chwast for inspiring a high standard of excellence: "It was very intimidating to see how much Seymour worked," he says. "He arrived before anyone and was always the last to leave." To explain his power of concentration, Chwast simply notes: "I just work until I get it right."

The working atmosphere was disciplined, but there was a buzz about it—with friends or family dropping by, messengers going in and out, and suppliers delivering art material. Thanks to articles in *Graphis* magazine, the studio was attracting the curiosity of graphic designers worldwide. Groups of foreign art students would come by, asking for permission to photograph everything—including drawings thrown in the trash can. Around bagels and coffee, there was endless talk about food, art, music, philosophy, and politics.

If a job was rejected by a client—which happened from time to time—the whole studio would break into a spontaneous rejection chant. Soon they were all dancing around the drawing boards, singing "re-jex-shion, re-jex-shion" to a Calypso tune. "There was a sense of delight," says Flood. "It was like a family." Once, a gray-suited student walked in to show his portfolio, only to find Glaser in his bathing suit, playing the banjo while talking on the phone.

Early on, an agent had been hired—someone with a couple of suits and a good command of the English language. A critical member of the team, he or she would drum up new business and deal with the specifics of each assignment. "You had to be able to defend the vision of the illustrator, even if it was different from the vision of the client," recalls Myrna Davis, who would sometimes second Jane Lander in her role as *femme d'artiste*. "The Push Pin illustrators didn't see themselves as hired guns," she explains. "They were fine artists who somehow were willing to subject themselves to the tension of solving someone else's problem—while still doing the work they wanted to do." Chwast agrees. "I have always tried to use my assignments as platforms for whatever I have to say, while the client, in turn, uses me."

To further simplify the work of designers and keep a high level of productivity throughout the day, a research assistant was dispatched to the New York Public Library on 42nd Street to find inspiring reference material. Acting as a divining rod, he or she would often return to the studio with unexpected iconographic loot. The research process was so stimulating that it became the basis of Push Pin's unique brand of historicism. Soon Glaser realized that these scraps of visual clichés were more revealing of a particular period than traditional historical analysis. As if accidentally, he began to integrate in his work obscure vernacular references to little known art forms: A piece on e.e. cummings was influenced by Japanese calligraphic washes; a record cover for Richard Strauss's *Don Quixote* would be inspired by Picasso drawings; the famous Dylan poster, which became an icon to the Sixties' generation, integrated a Marcel Duchamp silhouette with Arabic design elements. "The study of cliché as a mode of expression is fundamental to an understanding of design," said Glaser in his interview with Peter Mayer. "Clichés are symbols or devices that have lost their power and magic; yet they persist because of some kind of essential truth."

Oklahoma-born Paul Davis, who came to New York in 1955 and joined Push Pin in 1959, remembers being swept off his feet by this constant flow of hybrid cultural stimulation. "Where I came from, people only collected stamps or comic books, but these people were different," he says. "Seymour and Milton were relentless foragers, always bringing to the studio wonderful products, ceramics, or labels from one place or another. Milton collected Indian miniatures, while Seymour collected Victorian children's books. There was so much stuff around that we had this fantasy about opening a store."

While the studio was a clearinghouse for ideas and artifacts, it was also a clearinghouse for people. "Everybody used Push Pin as a starting point to develop significant careers," says Glaser. Two of the original founders, Sorel and Ruffins, left after a couple of years to work on their own, the first as a major political satirist, the second as a children's book illustrator. Chwast and Glaser remained sole owners, hiring illustrators either as staff or as featured artists with star billing in the Push Pin dramatis personae. In two decades, between 1954 and 1974, more than 20 people contributed their formidable personalities and talents to Push Pin's reputation. Many, like Glaser, Chwast, Ruffins, and Sorel, were Cooper Union alumni. Among them were John Alcorn, Vincent Ceci, Herb Levitt, George Leavitt, Norman Green, and Loring Eutemey. Others came from some of the best schools in the country: Jason McWhorter, Tim Lewis, and Paul Davis were graduates of the School of Visual Arts; Jerry Smokler and James McMullan graduated from Pratt Institute; Isadore Seltzer from the Art Center in Los Angeles; Cosmos Sarchiapone from Columbia University; Jerry Joyner from California College of Arts and Crafts; Sam Antupit from the Yale School of Architecture and Design. Haruo Miyauchi, a graduate of design schools in Japan, joined Push Pin as an intern and returned to Japan several years later as an accomplished artist. Barry Zaid, who stayed at Push Pin six years, was a self-taught illustrator, but he had studied archaeology and art history at the University of Toronto. "It's hard to go back and look at the work we did then," he says. "You can't help but feel nostalgic. Push Pin was so irresistible—yet, sooner or later, we all had to move on."

What kept the studio together was the meeting of those two remarkable men, Milton Glaser and Seymour Chwast. One could hardly imagine two people more patently dissimilar yet more philosophically compatible. "Milton would propose and Seymour would resist," says James McMullan, who met them just before they made their first down payment on the 32nd Street town house. "But it infallibly worked out. They got things done this way." Sitting back to back at their respective drawing boards in the middle of the studio, Glaser and Chwast were a study in contrasts.

Glaser is the optimist. "I have never experienced hardship at work," he says. "My mind doesn't work that way. I have always been interested in the creation of pleasure, the creation of interest." Even when the going got tough—when, for example, imitators like Peter Max or Heinz Edelmann received the acclaim Glaser deserved—he would gracefully concede. "I couldn't have done what they did. And I am grateful for what I have done," he'd say earnestly. The soul of fairness, Glaser is such a likable character, it's almost alarming. No wonder he is a mentor figure to successive generations of students, peers, and clients.

Unlike Glaser, who works with ease, Chwast works against the grain—starting at seven in the morning and stopping only when he "gets it right." Watercolor and delicate pen work aren't his favorite mediums. He prefers to do battle with ballpoint pens, colored pencils, chisels, wood, metal, and cardboard. He intentionally uses a primitive style to slow down his hand and make sure that his deftness does not get ahead of his mind. "The concept has always been most important," he says in the introduction to his 1985 book, *The Left-Handed Designer*. "Surface, neatness, rendering, and craft are things that interest me less." A strained rusticity betrays his odd ambivalence, as if he meant to encourage his subject matter to resist being objectified on the page.

The coming together of Glaser and Chwast had been a transformational event; their coming apart was just as momentous. In a way, their split, made official in 1974, was a reaffirmation of what they had always believed—namely, that you can't remain creative if you become entrapped in your own image. It happened slowly. First, Push Pin illustrators began to win gold medals, accolades, and honorary positions; sometimes, 25 percent of the awards in a show were presented to members of the studio. Then, numerous articles and profiles appeared in prestigious magazines like *Graphis*, *Idea*, *Communication Arts*, and even *Newsweek*. Last but not least, Push Pin's alumni—Paul Davis and James McMullan, in particular—contributed to the legend by becoming extremely successful on their own.

Davis, who is as much a painter as he is a designer, was doing posters, book jackets, and album covers that were the subjects of numerous museum retrospectives worldwide. Eventually, he served as art director of Joseph Papp's New York Shakespeare Festival and Public Theater between 1984 and 1991. McMullan gained tremendous visibility with his journalistic illustrations for magazines and for his posters for the Lincoln Center Theater. Like Davis's paintings, McMullan's watercolors became an integral part of the New York cultural scene.

In 1970, there was a major retrospective at the Louvre's Musée des Arts Décoratifs, followed by an exhibition in London. It was an unprecedented achievement: for the first time, illustrators were treated like real artists. The French press was raving. "The most brilliant graphic art team in the world," wrote *Le Nouvel Observateur*. "When one goes to see the Push Pin show, one's vision is cleansed, and one's spirit refreshed," said *Le Figaro*. "Push Pin is a Renaissance force in graphics," proclaimed *La Dépêche du Midi*.

To Glaser, these accomplishments and flattering headlines read like the writing on the wall. "I felt that we were lodged in history," he now says. "We had become a cultural commodity. Because I was interested in more than what Push Pin was becoming known for, I had to leave." Twenty years after he founded Push Pin, Milton Glaser walked away from it. His sudden freedom gave him a chance to increase his involvement with *New York*, a weekly he had founded with Clay Felker in 1968, and to form Milton Glaser Inc., a design consultancy handling a wide range of disciplines, from corporate identity programs to interior design. Later, in 1983, he teamed with Walter Bernard to create WBMG, a firm specializing in editorial design.

Without losing any momentum, Chwast took full ownership of the Push Pin Studios, continuing to publish the newsletter—renamed *Push Pin Graphic*—with as much inventiveness as if it were a full-fledged literary magazine. Issues like "New York at Night," "What is This Thing Called Love?," "Going to Hell," and "Mothers" are classics, displaying Push Pin's verve at its best. In 1982, Chwast joined with Steven Heller to produce books, principally on graphic design. "We would meet late at night and come up with intriguing themes, like New Jersey or Johann Sebastian Bach's birthday," recalls Heller. "Eventually, some of them would become illustrated books." As much an author as he is a designer, Chwast can't help but be himself in everything he does. His phenomenal prolificness is a measure of his wits. In 1995, D.K. Holland joined the renamed Pushpin Group as a partner, while Chwast remains its director.

And so, almost 50 years after the first *Push Pin Almanack* came off the press, the Push Pin spirit flourishes—its spelling now "Pushpin," but its pictorial message still germane to the times. "The architects of the Push Pin 'style' have hardly bothered to look back," wrote CBS creative director Lou Dorfsman on the occasion of Push Pin's 15th anniversary. "They have continued to refine their techniques and increase their powers, so that, while the world of American graphics may have at times seemed to be 'drowning in Push Pin,' Glaser, Chwast, and their fertile crew were always safely somewhere else."

What happens when illustrations become icons
More often than not, the work of
top illustrators is used to
support the image of the people who
hire them—not to inform, expose, startle,
clarify, or, God forbid, illustrate.

10

As I unwrapped *The Century of Sex, Playboy's History of the Sexual Revolution*, a gift from my husband for Christmas, I heard myself say "Fun! I can't wait to look at the illustrations." When it comes to sex, all things being equal, pictures are more interesting than text.

Anyone who is old enough to remember *The Joy of Sex* knows what I mean. Originally published in 1972, this landmark how-to book contained more than 100 explicit illustrations by Charles Raymond and Christopher Foss. Before the end of the decade, it sold more than ten million copies. The anatomically correct yet surprisingly elegant drawings had an irresistible voyeuristic appeal. You couldn't help but stare at them, their pristine renderings emphasizing the subversive content of the visual information.

But that was then, and this is now. To my grave disappointment, my 548-page *Playboy* history book had no illustrations—only a handful of color reproductions showing vintage movie posters and magazine covers. What a bummer! I expected something a little more graphic from Hugh Hefner. I should have known better. Today the medium of illustration is seldom used to stir controversy. Most art directors think of it as an extension of graphic design—visuals as punctuation for the eye.

In fact, illustration and graphic design, two rather different specialties, are today merging into one and the same thing. More and more designers, inspired by the likes of Robynne Raye, Charles Anderson, James Victore, Michael Mabry, and Paula Scher are honing their illustration skills. At the same time, more and more illustrators are emulating Milton Glaser, Mirko Ilic, Paul Davis, and Seymour Chwast, and are opening their own design studios.

Paradoxically, as the line between graphic design and illustration is blurred, both disciplines gain definition. By joining forces, graphic designers and illustrators produce work that's more focused and visible. The trend is profitable to illustrators in particular. They are brought into the creative process earlier, their signature style now considered an "integral component of the visual strategy." Illustrators who used to think that $500 was fair compensation for their editorial spots can now look forward to signing lucrative contracts to do advertising, packaging, or advertorial campaigns for major corporate clients.

But there's more to this than meets the eye. With more work for illustrators out there, the chances of making a culturally significant contribution have almost disappeared. In 1993, when *The New Yorker* featured a cover illustration by Art Spiegelman of a racially mixed couple kissing, the publishing world went ballistic. Even *Playboy* has become too much of an institution these days to gamble its reputation on some controversial graphic expression. Ironically, Istvan Banyai, who illustrates for *Playboy* on a regular basis, does some of his most conservative work for the magazine that is often credited with spawning the sexual revolution. "Of all my clients, it's not *Playboy*, but Merriam Webster, the dictionary people, who published some of my most racy work," he says. "For a modest paperback book titled *The Slang of Sin*, they let me go over the edge. I was surprised. Maybe they didn't look closely at my drawings."

More often than not, the work of today's best illustrators is used to support the image of the people who hire them—not to inform, expose, startle, clarify, or, God forbid, illustrate. As a result, few illustrations stand on their own anymore. You seldom find yourself studying a drawing, scrutinizing its details to extract all the nuances of the visual information. More likely, you judge its impact in context, as part of the cultural environment.

"This illustration looks like a champagne ad," said a client at a recent editorial meeting where artwork for a book his company was sponsoring was being discussed. It was quite perceptive of him, indeed. Illustrator Anja Kroencke had done a series of ads for Freixenet, a fancy Spanish sparkling wine. I kept pulling more examples of illustrations for him to review. "Nope, this one says Bendel to me," he remarked. "This other one is very

Dooney & Bourke. Oh, I like this next one—unfortunately, it reminds me of the Stila cosmetics packaging." At long last, one illustrator met his approval. "Let's not work with her," interrupted the art director. "She is too difficult. She's got a mind of her own."

A mind (especially a confident and creative one) is a terrible thing to waste. In the mid-1990s, French illustrator Jean-Philippe Delhomme became the toast of the town when he won the Barneys advertising campaign account. His witty illustrations epitomized the ultrachic downtown fashion scene of the time. Overnight, offers for high-profile packaging, CD covers, brochures, and ads came pouring in. "I was terrified," he told me. "This was the end of me. I was branded!" As soon as his contract with Barneys expired, Delhomme went into virtual hiding, refusing to work for another U.S. client. Now a well-established illustrator in France, he is still leery of having his work overexposed in the United States.

This fear of being typecast has haunted the acting profession for years, and illustrators are finding out that developing a new persona once you've had a successful role is a daunting task. A growing number of European illustrators are confronting this situation. Snatched up by everyone as soon as they burst on the scene (young English illustrator Graham Rounthwaite, who did Levi's rebellious Silver Tab campaign, is one of them), they not only get branded, they also attract a bevy of cheap imitators. Making matters worse, as soon as they become icons, their illustrations, however provocative, lose their ability to delight, intrigue, or even offend the viewer. They only serve as a reminder of the brand imagery they've helped create.

"You have to remain impulsive," says Istvan Banyai, whose work is popular without being branded. "I can't be nailed because clients never know for sure what to expect from me. I never know what I am going to do either. I am the first to be surprised. I am saved by my own inconsistencies." Or, as imperious fashion editor Diana Vreeland used to say, "Give them what they never knew they wanted." In other words: Stay ahead of the curve.

When illustrators trust their ability to surprise and be surprised, it can work wonders. Recently, a small illustration by Banyai in *The New Yorker* caught me off-guard. For a wry article by Christopher Buckley on how parents have trouble meeting the demands of their kids' homework, he drew a small child overwhelmed by the weight of her knapsack piled high with the props of her science projects. While Buckley's prose was fast and sleek, Banyai's drawing was charming and whimsical. It was an odd combination—two very different takes on a parental situation—but the friction between the two visions produced a small yet auspicious spark. That spark—that brief illumination—is the sign of a good illustration. To illustrate (*in* + *lustrare*) means "to make bright." Let this set the standard.

In search of modularity

Modular furnishing revealed itself to be too
cumbersome for everyday residential use.
It looked better in pictures than in reality.
Modular furnishing, in fact, was
popular mostly with movie stars.

The Holy Grail. The Fountain of Youth. Perpetual Motion. Behind these notions lies a simple truth: It takes a mortal to invent the concept of Eternity. The American version of the Quest is the Pursuit of Happiness. The Italians, since the days of the Romans, strive for Artistic Perfection. My uncle, an architect, is obsessed with the Greeks' Golden Section. He believes in Absolute Geometry. When he was young, he tried to invent the Universal Box.

"It could be a chair, a table, a container, a bucket, or a hat," he used to tell me. "Multiply the box and you can build the most beautiful house. Subdivide it and you can design anything—a spoon, a lamp, even a pair of shoes." He would draw a square on a piece of paper and show me all you can do with that one perfect shape. Stacked, twisted, folded, cut, or angled, the same square would dance in front of my eyes and turn into a cube, a spiral, a cylinder, or a pyramid. As nimble as a cartoon character, the rigid square was capable of a life of its own.

A fervent Modernist, my uncle thought that modular design, with its rigorous aesthetic, would help us solve the problems of the world. Production problems: One single mold could be used to manufacture hundreds of products. Communication problems: One unique range of sizes would minimize explanations and mistakes. Cultural problems: A shared passion for geometry would provide the basis for a universal language system. He was—and still is—turned toward the future. References to the past annoy him. I remember him stripping the ornate ceiling moldings, scrollwork, and decorative window frames in his eighteenth-century apartment in Paris. He tried to convince my mother (his sister) to tear down the "ugly" fifteenth-century fireplace with its "obscene" caryatids in the dilapidated manor she had acquired in the South of France. But unlike the *Mon Oncle* character in the famous Jacques Tati film, my uncle loathes trendy modern gadgetry. Heir to the Bauhaus tradition, he is a builder-philosopher, a poet of numbers, and a purist. He is a Le Corbusier fan.

The visionary French-Swiss architect Le Corbusier developed what he called the Modulor (Modul-or, i.e., Golden Module), a proportional system based on modular subdivisions that allowed him to design an infinite number of harmonious architectural variations on a single mathematical theme. Although he is regarded as one of the founders of modern architecture, Le Corbusier's theories are very different from what we now call modular thinking. Most contemporary modular systems today are based on the multiplication of identical units, resulting in a repetitive pattern. Le Corbusier's Modulor is based on a division—the theoretical division of the human figure into its proportionate components. "To anyone but a Frenchman this sort of [distinction] might seem pedantic in the extreme," noted Peter Blake in his 1976 book *The Master Builders*. "Indeed, anyone but a Frenchman would probably be incapable of achieving a Modulor system."

Following in my uncle's footsteps, I studied architecture. I went to the Beaux-Arts school in Paris, hoping to discover the secret of the Golden Section. But in the early 1960s, Le Corbusier (Corbu for the initiates) was still considered an *enfant terrible* in French academic circles. Modernity was frowned upon. Instead of studying mathematics, I was forced to design dainty neo-classical buildings—Baroque gazebos, Italian palaces, and Victorian pavilions. I spent hours learning to draw details of the Ionic, Doric, and Corinthian columns my uncle was so busy tearing down, both literally and figuratively. In the middle of my second year I took a semester off and came to New York. It was, of course, a revelation.

Forget the subtle geometry of abstract spatial relationships, the aesthetic beauty of pure forms, and the intellectually satisfying ordinance of the Golden Section. This place was wild, intoxicating, and overwhelming—this place was a modular jungle. I fell in love with New York because it was a faulty mathematical proposition. It was more than the sum of its parts. The sheer power of chaotic multiplication swept me off my feet.

Modular design American-style is almost a negation of its European counterpart. "Corbu became convinced that some 'American gangsters' were trying to steal his Modulor by setting up a company called something like Modular Structures," recalls Blake in *The Master Builders*. "When Corbu showed the Modulor to the late Albert Einstein, in Princeton, Einstein told him that this was 'a range of dimensions which makes the bad difficult and the good easy.' " What Le Corbusier did not understand—and what Einstein very diplomatically did not tell him—is that the universal appeal of American design is its cheerful lack of pretension. In America, the bad is easy and the good is difficult. We all love Manhattan, although we all know that for one elegantly designed Seagram Building, we have to endure dozens of gaudy superstructures.

"Modern" architecture in America is not a native phenomenon. Left to themselves, American architects are quite lyrical. Louis Sullivan's decorative Art Nouveau and Frank Lloyd Wright's vernacular Prairie Style are genuine examples of truly American modernism. If architects like Mies van der Rohe and Marcel Breuer had not emigrated to the United States, Sixth Avenue today would probably be a different boulevard—a visionary concourse right out of the 1893 World's Columbian Exposition in Chicago.

Like modern American architecture, American modular furniture is not strictly an American invention. The idea was popularized in the States a full 20 years after Marcel Breuer's first modular prototypes had been produced at the Dessau Bauhaus school in Germany. In 1946, Harvey Prober, a self-taught designer with a small Brooklyn factory, introduced what he called a "nuclear" seating group. But his modular furniture was nothing like Breuer's austere tubular steel designs. His version was user-friendly, featuring concave, convex, rectangular, wedge-like, and circular upholstered sections. It was an instant sensation. The postwar years had signaled the end of the so-called glamorous 1940s. The 1950s, synonymous with middle-class prosperity, were going to be casual, open-ended, and easy. The American public, at long last, seemed ready for "modern" innovations.

Modular furniture suggests faith in the future. Acknowledging a need for flexible seating arrangement implies that you welcome potential change. Harvey Prober sold a concept rather than a thing—versatility, choice, options. But modular furnishing revealed itself to be too cumbersome for everyday residential use. It looked better in pictures than in reality. Magazines featured trendy interiors with curved sectional sofas wrapped like lazy snakes around storage cabinets, planters and coffee tables; advertisements showed formidable wall units incorporating entertainment centers, color television sets, and full bars. But for most Americans, this was too radical a change. Modular furnishing, in fact, was mostly popular with movie stars.

So, while few individuals were able to handle the challenge of modularity, corporations thrived on it. With the addition of partitions, shelves, file cabinets, optional features, and easy upgrades, modular units, a.k.a contract furniture, quickly became synonymous with the office environment. As businesses were booming, so were the contract furniture companies. Knoll, Herman Miller, Steelcase, and Stendig became industry leaders by defining modular designs with a strong signature style.

The rise of a mid-managerial class in the U.S. in the 1960s and 1970s parallels the development of a modular mentality. But the return to individual values and the glorification of personal greed in the 1980s heralded the end of pure geometry. The postmodern movement, with its eccentric sense of history, was first and foremost an anti-modular trend—in other words, it was an anti-middle-class trend. When fake marble columns, pseudo-cornices, and mock porticos became standard features in corporate headquarters across America, I knew that misfortune was in the air. The new office environment, complete with metal palm trees and faux gazebos, looked like a theatrical set. I had the feeling that we were preparing the stage for the last act of a tragic play. And indeed the Reagan years delivered the *coup de grâce*—today the American Dream is but a shadow lurking behind the corporate scene.

During the postmodern years I kept wondering how my uncle—a man who used to break into hives in the presence of fake wood—was surviving in this strange anti-architectural climate. But I was too busy to track him down. Finally, I found the time to visit him in his newly renovated house in the Vallée de Chevreuse, an exclusive suburb outside of Paris. Every home in the quaint village of Gif-sur-Yvette, where he now lives, had been restored to recapture its original turn-of-the-century picturesque charm. My uncle's house, at the end of a quiet alley, was whitewashed and unassuming. I rang the bell. He came to the door, a 6' 6" giant with thinning white hair, clad in a pair of blue industrial overalls. Behind him the house glowed like the inside of an empty seashell. It had been gutted out to bare its modest structural soul—a straight staircase, a simple fireplace, a couple of walls. It was furnished with modular furniture, elegant prototypes that were, as far as I could tell, his latest variations of the Universal Box. I noticed a large table, eight cleverly designed chairs, a discreet wall unit, and two comfortable lounge chairs. The overall impression was almost medieval—yet pristine.

We had a lot of catch-up to do. But my uncle, a practical man, wanted to talk about joints. "Modular design does not work in most cases because designers don't understand how to make joints," he told me. "Not just physical joints, but functional joints as well." I had to sit straight and conjure up my wits. We spent the rest of the afternoon trying to define the shape of things to come. What is the difference between interior space and exterior space? What makes more sense, proportions or harmonic relationships? What is most useful, "finalized" or "non-finalized" objects?

When I left his house—a veritable laboratory of modularity—I felt I was going back into a world obsessed with its past, a world reluctant to imagine Tomorrow. I was confused as well. It was as if this visit had taken me back in time, to the glorious days of the Bauhaus. It is paradoxical indeed, but when we try to imagine a futuristic environment, we unconsciously conjure up concepts and images that originated in Germany in the 1920s. But maybe there is a new future out there after all. We just turned a corner into the third millennium. That corner is a joint—a link, a nexus, a junction. I held my breath. For a brief moment I was able to visualize the present moment as an in-between space, a joint linking two modular golden sections of the future.

Object lesson #2: the coffee table
When leisure was promoted not only as
something to enjoy but also something to
consume, the odd tray table changed
function and became an adjunct to the
couch—a footstool, really. Thus was born
the coffee table as we know it.

12

Some people remember the first time they saw the sea, the Eiffel Tower, or the northern lights. I don't remember anything of that scope, but I do remember the first time I saw a coffee table. The year was 1962.

From a distance it looked like a thick piece of glass precariously propped on skinny chrome legs. As I moved closer to examine it, my perspective changed, and the clear slab became a mirror reflecting the living room upside down. Through this looking glass I could see a window framing a rectangular piece of the Manhattan skyline that appeared to be anchored to the thick carpet.

"I hate those fingerprints" said the woman who owned this strange object. As she kneeled, trying to erase some offending smudges with the edge of her sleeves, I sensed her utter devotion. Perhaps she was praying to the icons of Good Taste on this altar: the thick glass ashtray, the burnished pewter cigarette box, the three issues of *House & Garden*, and the small sculpture, a Henry Moore study of a reclining nude. I had arrived from Paris that afternoon, and this was my first visit to an American home. Driving into New York from the airport, I'd had a premonition that from now on anything could happen; a windswept newspaper had taken off vertically from the sidewalk and disappeared above the rooftops, and streets were venting steam like fumaroles near a volcano.

My first coffee table was part of this new phantasmagoric backdrop. That day, invited to sit down by the coffee table, I sank far into the soft upholstery of the couch, experiencing an unexpected change of perspective as the horizon rose drastically around me. From this low angle things at long last looked almost normal. Maybe to understand America I would need a new point of view, a parallax adjustment—maybe to appreciate this new culture I would always have to sit 13 inches from the ground.

As unbelievable as it may seem now, I had never seen a coffee table—even though one of the very first ones had been designed in 1927 by a French furniture designer, Jean-Michel Frank, who created it for the much acclaimed Paris residence of the Vicomte de Noailles. But this original concept remained behind privileged doors for a long time. The average French family was not about to throw away their antique wing chairs and matching side tables for furniture that not only looked too low but also too bulky. When Frank immigrated to the United States in the mid-1930s, he updated his earlier idea into what was to become another American classic, the Parsons table.

On this side of the Atlantic, the first examples of coffee tables can be found in shelter magazines as early as 1925. Although they are the right height, the things, looking like flimsy trays with legs attached, stand at least four feet away from the couch. They are nonetheless coffee tables, not the traditional tea tables, and are displayed as such, complete with distinctive silver coffee sets. For the next couple of decades, the tray-on-legs contraptions were favorite wedding gift items. But no amount of styling—"Queen Anne," "French Provincial," "Italian Renaissance," "English Restoration," "Chinese Dynasty," or "Colonial"—will get people to move these early coffee tables closer to the couch. They are still considered "occasional" tables, something to be kept at a respectable distance, like a servant waiting in the wings. Only in the 1950s, when prosperous Americans learned to relax their posture, sit back, and put their feet up on the sofa, did the coffee table come within arm's-length of the couch. Indeed, only after World War II, when leisure was promoted not only as something to enjoy but also something to consume, would the odd tray table change function and become an adjunct to the couch—a footstool, really—to allow people to recline and grab their drinks and snacks without getting up.

Casual relaxation, which combines drinking, eating, and lounging, is unique to this culture. Although I wanted to adopt the American Way of Life, as epitomized by Coca-Cola ads showing teens noshing between meals in semi-horizontal positions, I couldn't bring myself to go limp on a couch while drinking or eating. My new American husband, whose idea of the good life was putting your feet up while reading a book, sipping coffee, and nibbling on salted peanuts, urged me to buy a coffee table. But I stubbornly rejected the kidney-shaped glass coffee table my dear mother-in-law innocently offered to buy for our first Upper East Side apartment. Undaunted by my refusal, she courageously tried to educate me. First she showed me a mahogany oval table with hinged flaps from Lord & Taylor, then a lacquered Chinese model from B. Altman. Getting no reaction, she suggested an ornate wrought iron creation a friend of hers could get at a decorator's discount. She even tried to interest me in three identical end tables I could push together or split off for buffet parties. To no avail. Raised with strict table manners, I would not—or could not—imagine owning a piece of furniture that encouraged me to slump and swallow at the same time.

For the first years of my marriage, I sat upright on the edge of the couch with my coffee cup aloft, straining to keep my knees locked together. At long last, my husband took the initiative and got a coffee table on his own. He chose a platform-planter combo with a thick marble top and even bought some ferns for it. It wasn't until after our divorce that I learned to be less judgmental, more flexible, and less controlling—especially when it came to my food issues.

One night, less than a year after I hit the singles scene, I felt a distinctive shift in my spine during dinner, and, unexpectedly, I slumped. It was a wonderful feeling, as if the world were my hammock. Feeling bold and experimental, the next day I settled on the couch sipping a soft drink without removing it from its brown paper bag. Not long after that, I sat on a stoop and ate cold pizza. It was only a matter of weeks before I would drag two crates into my little apartment and put together a makeshift coffee table.

Only then did it dawn on me that the coffee table is not a

functional object—on the contrary it's a *tabula rasa*, a blank tablet on which each individual can write his or her definition of comfort and relaxation. Whether you let junk gather on it—the Sunday papers, empty Chinese food cartons, socks, and sneakers—or keep it clutter free, safe for a few tasteful collectibles, the coffee table is a no-pressure zone.

You have to go all the way back to the fifth century B.C., to Mesopotamia and Greece, where wealthy people ate while reclining, to find tables in front of couches. But this arrangement, in which revelers lean on one elbow while eating with their fingers, doesn't look particularly comfortable. There are also rare examples during the Renaissance of similar contraptions. In paintings of the period, the presence of a low table in a room always suggests a sense of ease. In Roger van der Weyden's famous *Annunciation*, the Virgin Mary, book in hand, leans casually on a bench covered by a shawl—a piece of furniture not unlike the narrow wooden coffee table popular in the 1940s. A couple of decades later, Vittore Carpaccio's *Dream of Saint Ursula* shows among the bedroom's furnishings a small knee-high table with what looks like an unfinished manuscript and a couple of books on it. In both instances, the tables are adorned with a shawl, a sign of casual comfort.

Otherwise, throughout Western history, tables remained about 28 inches from the ground, while ottomans, camp stools, chests, and benches vary in style and size and seem to give people a lot of comfort and delight. Steeped in exoticism, the nineteenth century is particularly fond of these versatile and movable objects, which are often festooned with fringes, tassels, handles, and cushions. It is the very eclecticism of these primitive coffee tables that makes them such enjoyable things to have.

Today, only a half-dozen coffee tables have achieved the status of classics. I think particularly of Mies van der Rohe's glass-top square design, Saarinen's low pedestal table for Knoll, and Noguchi's 1944 glass and wood sculpture. This limited selection of elegant coffee tables should come as no surprise: What makes coffee tables unique is not what they are—multipurpose handy platforms—but what they are not. They are not defined by their function. So close to the ground, they are quintessentially awkward, stuck in an artistic limbo where they must struggle for aesthetic recognition.

The appeal of coffee tables is not their fine design, either. They are a product of Pop culture, kitsch objects that bring out the whimsical side of a designer. The best among them look like odd sculptures. They are that thing in the middle of the living room that looks like a cross between a guitar, a boomerang, a flying saucer, a turtle, a sleigh, and a mushroom.

Extracting the essence of a magazine
Usually, a perfume starts from a simple idea.
That idea can be a word, a feeling—or a
magazine. I was once given the assignment
of extracting the essence of a women's
magazine and translating it into a scent.

Serendipitous olfactory sidebars, the now ubiquitous magazine scent strips, with their pry-'n'-peel and scratch-'n'-sniff actions, have become part of the subliminal editorial message. As a result, there is a natural affinity between magazines and fragrances. So no one was surprised when, during an editorial meeting at *Mirabella* magazine, I proposed to investigate what it would take to create a real fragrance with the same personality—and the same name—as the magazine.

I got the assignment. My mandate was to find out if it was possible, in fact, to extract the essence of a magazine and translate it into a scent. I was to ask trend-forecasters, graphic designers, bottle makers, and perfumers—the same professionals who routinely create fragrances for luxury clients—to convert *Mirabella* into an olfactory experience. What steps would they take—and would it be different from what they do for their other clients?

None of the experts I called seem to think that my request was strange. Today, fashion designers like Donna Karan, cosmetics giants like Revlon, jewelers like Bulgari and Cartier, cobblers like Gucci, glassmakers like Lalique—and of course celebrities like Elizabeth Taylor and Michael Jordan—routinely create fragrances that capture their persona. In the fragrance industry, a rose by any other name is still a rose.

First, the idea. Usually, a perfume starts from a simple concept. That idea can be an object, a word, a feeling, or a real person. Amarige, by Givenchy, was inspired by a gold organza evening blouse designed by Hubert de Givenchy: Like the garment, the scent is exuberant and romantic. Parfum d'été, a sun-drenched fragrance by Kenzo, is the expression of a single word, "summer," the designer's favorite season. Cherish, by Revlon, was developed after consumers in focus groups told market researchers that what mattered most to them was spending quality time with their loved ones. Pleasures, by Lauder, was dedicated to the lovely Aerin, Estée Lauder's granddaughter.

The point of departure for the magazine's fictitious fragrance was "The *Mirabella* Woman." But who, really, is this smart, stylish, independent *Mirabella* reader—someone, research tells us, who spends more than $100 on perfumes and colognes a year? The answer to this question came from Desgrippes Gobé Associates (DGA), an international design firm responsible for positioning and packaging fragrances for clients like Boucheron, Cartier, Patou, Prada, Ann Taylor, Laura Biagotti, and Victoria's Secret.

DGA's Creative director Peter Levine, an inspired trend-forecaster, took over this part of the project. He asked for back issues of *Mirabella*. "I figure out trends by sifting through thousands and thousands of pictures," he says, "I don't probe them, I just react emotionally." In less than an hour, he had reviewed more than 50 issues. "I look for images with a 'smell'—images that suggest a scent to me," he explains. "I tear them and throw them in different piles on the floor. The trick is to bypass the mind."

This particular methodology is unique to DGA. There is more than one way to find out who the potential customer is. To develop Trueste, by Tiffany, design director John Loring only had to look at the people who enter the Fifth Avenue store. He didn't need a marketing maven to tell him that they were in search of something special—a wedding ring, a gift, an engraved invitation—something to express their "truest" feelings. In contrast, Fabien Baron, the creative genius who designed the cK One bottle and advertising campaign for Calvin Klein, only tried to please his friends, all young models and trendy photographers.

Levine discovered who the "*Mirabella* Woman" was after staring at the pictures he had torn from the magazines. "At long last, it hit me like a ton of bricks," he recalls. "I was trying hard to create a single portrait of her, when I realized that she is a study in contrasts. She is both cool and warm. That's what makes her modern. Maybe she wears a cool navy suit, but she wears it directly on her skin. She is a minimalist, but she'll pin one fabulous piece of jewelry on her lapel. She sits in a slick steel chair, but her desk is made of natural blond wood." Using a half-dozen magazine tear-sheets, he created a composite of the ideal Mirabella Woman: a multifaceted individual with a cool/warm personality. This collage became the central concept that would inspire the packaging designer and the perfumer.

Next, we needed to shape the abstraction. Kenneth Hirst, head of product design at DGA, started to work on the bottle. "The worst thing for a designer is to try to second-guess the client," he says. "This cool/warm positioning lets me come up with creative solutions. I have a focus, but no restrictions." "Cool," for him, was the glass, which he decided should be shaped like a prism, to emphasize luminosity. "Warm" was the fragrance—but also the stopper, which he imagined should look like a piece of rough amber.

With his partner Joël Desgrippes in Paris, Marc Gobé, president of DGA, has been involved with the launching of more than 50 fragrances worldwide. He wanted to push the initial concept as far as it would go. "Cool/warm suggests a back and forth movement," he told Hirst. "The Mirabella Woman is always on the move. We need to design a scent that goes back and forth—wherever she goes. The bottle should be interactive: more like a desk accessory than a decoration for her boudoir."

In close collaboration with model-maker George Utley (the man who crafted the final prototype for Elizabeth Taylor's White Diamonds perfume bottle), Hirst set out to make the bottle interactive: "I decided the container had to do more than simply hold its content," he explained. Shaped like an inverted cone, with a pointed apex, the transparent vial he created looks like a cross between a prism and a spinning top. It sits on the desk at an angle, without rolling all over the place. Nudge it slightly, and it does a complete revolution on itself. "There is no fussiness," says Hirst. "Just the contrast between the cool glass and the warm amber stopper. It is definitely something you would like to play with while talking on the phone."

Perfume bottles as playthings are gaining popularity. They are giving Daniel Rachmanis, president of SGD Glass, New York, quite a headache: "We are being challenged right and left to make bottles with impossible shapes," he says. Probably the world's largest manufacturer of cosmetic bottles and jars, SGD Glass recently solved the technological idiosyncrasies of Donna Karan's Chaos, Guerlain's Champs Elysées, and Elizabeth Arden's Fifth Avenue.

After the container comes the content. Of course, the scent is the deciding factor in the success of a fragrance. Called "juice," in industry jargon, a modern perfume can be years in the making. Unlike Chanel No. 5, which, legend has it, was perfumer Ernest Beaux's fifth sample, Allure by Chanel was No. 819, suggesting that the company went through at least that many samples before selecting the right one. At Tiffany, Vice President Susan Sussman spent two years comparing the submissions of three competing perfume manufacturers in order to create Trueste. "It takes much, much longer to come up with the juice than the packaging," she says.

Creating a fragrance can only be compared with writing a symphony. The perfumer (a.k.a. the nose) orchestrates olfactory notes that interact with each other like musical notes—the various rates of evaporation of the molecules in the fragrance providing an infinite number of subtle modulations.

At Revlon, a 20-person R&D team is constantly at work, testing juices in search of the next winning composition. "You cannot know what the consumer likes unless you talk to her," explains Steven Perelman, vice president of fragrance marketing, who worked on the Cherish project. "How else would you know that some fruity notes, like apple or peach, remind her of her favorite food?"

The natural choice to create the juice for Mirabella was International Flavors and Fragrances (IFF), one the world's largest suppliers of scents for perfumes, beauty products, shampoos, detergents, candles, and potpourris. The nose assigned to the project was senior perfumer Carlos Benaim, who is responsible for Polo, Eternity for Men, Elizabeth Taylor's White Diamonds, and Carolina Herrera for Women, among others. "All we can do in a couple of weeks is explore the cool/warm concept," he warned. "In real life, it takes at least a year of experiments, shuffles, and adjustments to finalize an olfactive idea."

In the 1980s, fragrances were warm, he explains. Recently, the trend has been toward cooler juices that break the traditional romantic (i.e. "warm") mold for perfumes. In 1996, there were no fewer than 15 fragrance launches with "nonseductive" positionings (i.e., "cool" scents). Among them were Allure, Dolce Vita, Pleasures, Trueste—all tantalizing scents that do not put the emphasis on romance. More and more women buy fragrances for themselves. "In focus group after focus group," says Perelman, "women told us that they didn't like advertisements suggesting that they were on the receiving end of a relationship."

Over the next few weeks, Benaim prepared a palette of warm and cool olfactory notes. Cool ones included green cucumber, mint, bergamot, lemony-fresh magnolia, and "Kasmiral," a synthetic ingredient as translucent as a voile. Warm ones were musk, honeysuckle, amber, rose and "Cashmeran," a comforting synthetic scent. And then, for good measure, he threw in the irresistible smell of a French plum called—what else—mirabelle.

"When you create a perfume, you have to let your mind wander," says Benaim. "Ultimately, the way people respond to scents is a mental construction made with olfactive impressions from their past." To test the notes, perfumers sprayed each other's bare arms, and the arms of their assistants, marking each spot with a pencil stroke. In the hallways of the IFF corporate headquarters—a very proper place—you often come across a group of people politely sniffing each other's skin. Repeated sniffs are mandatory—every 20 minutes or so—to check the various rates of evaporation.

In spite of all the science and chemistry involved—IFF

employs 50 PhDs in its lab—fragrance remains a subjective business. "In different people, the same note will trigger a wide range of associations," says Benaim. "Reaching a consensus can be tricky. But eventually—after everyone changes his or her mind back and forth at least three times—we can write down the formulation of a fragrance the way a doctor writes a prescription."

The *Mirabella* fragrance that emerged from this process was part of what Bob Brady, president of Parfums Givenchy, calls the Happy Trend. "To be modern, a scent doesn't have to be esoteric and serious," he says. Benaim agrees: "Sensual—not overtly sexy." His submission for *Mirabella* is cool at first—with notes of bergamot, rose, and freshly mown lawn rising through a discreet veil of lemony magnolia. This transparent screen never completely evaporates, only partially lifts to reveal a mouth-watering combination of mirabelle plum and musk.

I asked how much this fragrance would cost. "You tell me," says Benaim. "With small adjustments, we can bring the price of a juice down. Or drive it up through the ceiling. The smell of money is only one of the many ingredients."

At long last, it all came together—the juice, the bottle, and the packaging, an elegantly crafted circular container designed by Levine. With a racy top sitting astride a cream-colored box, it was definitely "happy." But the interior of this stylish *coffret* was a delicate, icy pale blue, a testament that cool and warm can indeed coexist in the best of all worlds. "Are we going to have scent strips?" I asked. In my mind's eye, I was already designing the advertising campaign.

Not a black and white issue
He looked a lot like a young Michael
Jackson with two gloves instead of
one—and like the African-American
rock 'n' roll star, he was split between
a black and a white identity.

14

The rodent, with its right hand holding the receiver as if it were a torch, is for me as much a symbol of freedom and hope as that other American icon, the Statue of Liberty. A classic, my 1976 deluxe push-button model is set, like Liberty, on a monumental base, his a large faux-wormy-walnut stand. Unlike more recent Mickey Mouse phones that are designed to be portable and compact (electronic Mickey keeps the receiver in his backpack), this telephone is heroic in proportions. Twelve inches tall, the cartoon character has presence. There is nothing tentative about him.

You can tell that the Disney people knew their Mickey—to draw him in action, and give him a believable personality, they had to first invent his physical attributes, which meant, among other things, establishing his precise weight, his exact flexibility, his buoyancy. As a result, whether flattened in drawings or silkscreened on T-shirts, printed on the face of a wristwatch, or molded in hard plastic, like my phone, his rubber-like body keeps its specificity.

My Mickey looks limber and springy. His ears stand up at an unequivocal angle. His snout sticks out expressively. His big head, angled sideways and upward as if to seek approval, throws his body off balance, and as a result his left leg is slightly bent. As any little boy would do when tilting his head to the left, Mickey has shifted his tongue to the right, instinctively re-establishing his sense of equilibrium. He looks vigorous, vibrant, and alive.

Unfortunately, my Mickey is physically fit but emotionally insecure. Sure, he is cheery with innocence and goodwill. He stands proudly, his left hand on his heart, holding the phone with the eagerness of a dog who just fetched his bone. But there is a questioning look on his face. Although there is enough room in the stand to house an answering machine, this Mickey is not the kind of fellow you would want to trust with your messages. "You deal with this call," says his body language. "You are a grown-up woman, I am just a dummy." I must have picked up the phone from him thousands of times over the last three decades, and as I talked, looked deeply into his trusting face before I could figure out what was behind that silly grin.

And then one day, it hit me: Under his oversized white mask, Mickey Mouse is hiding the body and the soul of a stereotypically mischievous little black boy. Created in 1928, decades before the Civil Rights movement, dark-skinned Mickey was conceived as an endearing little rascal, a scamp who plays tricks on others. Far from being the symbol of respectability he is now, he was a street kid. In cartoon after cartoon, he was cast as a jack-of-all-trades, a jazz musician, a comedian, a grocery boy, an aviator. He had stolen Charlie Chaplin's oversized shoes and Step'n Fetchit's white gloves. In fact he looked a lot like a young Michael Jackson with two gloves instead of one—and like the African-American rock 'n' roll star, he was split between a black and a white identity. But back then, race was not an issue for white folks. What mattered were his youth and energy. He inherited an enterprising personality from his creator, the 26-year-old Walt Disney.

By the mid-thirties, Mickey Mouse had become a national hero. But as he gained in popularity, he had to be sanitized and made palatable to a mainstream audience that rejected diversity and differences: Whenever he misbehaved too much in a cartoon, angry letters from irate viewers would arrive at the Walt Disney Studio. So his personality was toned down. As Mickey learned to become a soulless goody two-shoes, other characters had to provide comic relief. Pluto, Donald Duck, and Goofy, troublemakers all, became his companions.

By the end of that decade, the Three Little Pigs, Snow White, and Pinocchio had been introduced by Disney Studio, and they took some more pressure off Mickey. A little later, Dumbo, Bambi, Cinderella, and Peter Pan were also added to the pageant. The rest is history. But no Prince Charming, Big Bad Wolf, or Fairy Godmother could ever replace Mickey.

It was ironic: A member of one of the most oppressed

SOMETHING TO BE DESIRED

minorities had become an all-American icon and the symbol of Disney's success. Trapped by his own notoriety, unable to evolve as a character, Mickey-the-troublemaker had to be terminated. "The Sorcerer's Apprentice," released in 1940 as part of *Fantasia*, was to be his testament. The symbolism of that now-classic animated film is chilling. It's the story of a young boy who is publicly humiliated for playing with a magic power he could not control. In the last scene, Mickey Mouse returns the magician's hat to his master the sorcerer, becoming de facto a deflated hero. The look on his face says it all. His dream is over. He has no more freedom, no more autonomy. The Wizard, Walt Disney, takes it all away. It's a cruel moment in cartoon history. From there on, Mickey will be cast as mere product, a commercial property.

Today, Mickey Mouse is a prisoner in his own kingdom. He walks the streets of Disneyland and Disney World under surveillance. The aging cartoon character is never allowed to speak. An appointed "minder," equipped with a walky-talky, "protects" him. Take his picture, but don't expect him to say anything. One word, and he loses his job.

But Mickey Mouse cannot really be silenced. His suppressed racial identity speaks volumes. He is on my phone. Take his call, please. He wants to talk to you. Hurry, before his minders disconnect your call.

Walter Landor: a pioneer
Called by his critics "the guy who puts
stripes on everything," Walter Landor
could layer colors over colors,
cartouches over cartouches, and stripes
over stripes like no one else.

O n a business trip in Japan in the early 1960s, Walter Landor and his young research analyst Mim Ryan stopped the car on the side of the road to admire a flowering bougainvillea tree. A dapper gentleman with a very European mustache, Landor was an admirer of all things visual, "from beautiful flowers to pretty women," remembers Ryan. "He got out of the car and I saw him bend over toward the fallen blossoms and pick what I thought was a delicate flower petal. But when he came back to the car, he was holding in his hand a discarded candy wrapper he had found on the sidewalk."

One of the most influential branding pioneers, Landor was already a well-known packaging designer at the time. From his small waterfront office in San Francisco, "a funny little place with a creaking staircase in the middle of the vegetable market," recalls Ryan, he had redesigned the Benson & Hedges cigarette packs, the Sapporo beer can, and the Kellogg's Corn Flakes cereal box—the famous one with the spoon and the rooster.

Landor was not a hands-on designer, but a creative visionary. Driven by a youthful curiosity, he saw possibilities in everything and everyone. "Products are made in a factory, but brands are created in the mind," he once said. His San Francisco design company, established in 1941, is credited for creating or repositioning some of the most ubiquitous consumer brands worldwide, including Del Monte (1965), Levi's (1968), Cotton Inc. (1973), Schaefer Beer (1975), Marlboro (1977), Frito-Lay (1980), Dole (1984), and Fuji Film (1987). He also single-handedly branded the commercial aeronautics field, designing the logos and corporate identities of Alitalia, British Airways, Japan Airlines, Delta Airlines, Cathay Pacific Airways, Varig Airlines, and Thai Airlines.

But one of the most enduring brands Landor created was himself. Though he retired in 1989, the company he founded is still the number-one choice for big business. "In our field, the Landor name is as big as Coca-Cola," says Cheryl Swanson, an authority in the branding field, slyly referring to another of

Landor's successes. "If it wasn't for Walter, none of us would be here today. He is the father of what we now call brand design packaging."

In contrast, when I told friends in the chauvinistic New York design world that I was researching a story on Landor, they dismissed him as "a regional artist," their attitude a holdover from the days when "there was no there there" west of Chicago, to paraphrase Gertrude Stein. It was only in the late 1970s, when Pentagram Design opened an office in San Francisco, and "the Michaels" (Michael Vanderbyl, Michael Cronan, Michael Mabry, and Michael Manwaring) called attention to the Bay Area by winning design award after design award, that Landor came up as a blip on the East Coast design establishment's radar.

Clay Timon, CEO of Landor Associates, believes that what made Walter Landor so hard to categorize was his uniqueness. "Part of Walter's brand appeal was that he never did what was expected. He never showed when you thought he would. He did things his way. And clients adored him." Forty years ago, long before anyone else, Landor sold himself as a brand. He was not a package designer with a house style, but a man with a unique approach to problem solving. "Landor would be tickled if he came back today," adds Timon. "He would see that, at long last, the corporate culture is catching up with his vision."

Today, on landor.com, his portrait is featured in an old-fashioned medallion. A benign Sigmund Freud look-alike, he sports the same trimmed white beard and natty three-piece suit—all subtle visual references to the fact that Landor, born Landauer in Munich, Germany in 1913, was not a San Francisco native but a refined European émigré. "Like me, Walter came from an assimilated, German Jewish family," says Irina Bosner, a close family friend. "He was the quintessential immigrant, absorbing the culture everywhere he went, yet never quite belonging anywhere."

In 1931, the young man was sent to England to pursue his art education. During his first year, he changed the spelling of his name when he happened upon a London street named after Walter Savage Landor, a nineteenth-century English writer. It was the first time, but not the last time, he would fix a name. During his life, he was often called upon by clients to come up with names for products, concepts, and brands. Today, Landor Associates is famous for its naming expertise—a highly sought-after skill in a world where big corporations must negotiate cultural nuances across international boundaries. Disney's "Touchstone," Delta's "SkyMiles," FedEx's "The World on Time," and AT&T's "Lucent," are some of the carefully scripted words recently created by Landor Associates.

With his new British name, Landor assumed a well-tempered English manner. Years later, in San Francisco, he would charm everyone with his so-called "distinctive European demeanor." This expression conveyed the slight confusion his friends, employees, and clients felt when trying to identify the specific ethnic origin of his natural warmth, his quiet urbanity, his low voice, his slight accent, and his impeccable elegance.

In England, where he enrolled in London University's Goldsmith College School of Art, Landor quickly outgrew his Munich design influences—Bauhaus but also Werkbunk, the German equivalent of the Arts and Crafts Movement. A quick study, at age 22 he became a founding partner, with Misha Black and Milner Gray, of Industrial Design Partnership (IDP), the first industrial design consultancy in England. In 1939, he came to the United States as part of the design team for the British Pavilion at New York's World's Fair. He fell in love with San Francisco while traveling across the country to familiarize him-self with contemporary American industrial design. Upon learning that there were no designers in northern California, he decided to colonize the region. "My father knew how to make every situation work for him," says his daughter Susan, who worked with him for years. "He realized that he could be suc-cessful in this town because he could have it both ways—a good life, one that blurs the line between work and play."

Landor drew people to him. Teaching at the California School of Fine Art (now CCAC) he attracted—and partied with—an artsy crowd of colleagues, students, painters, architects, and sculptors. Among them were his future wife, Josephine, still an artist today, and painters like Mark Rothko and Richard Diebenkorn, then unknown. "It was a struggle right from the beginning," remembers Jo Landor. They married in 1940 and at first worked together from an apartment on Russian Hill. The couple had two daughters, Susan and Lynn. Early on, Walter decided that his specialty would be packaging. "He realized that he had a natural talent for designing things that appealed to the masses," recalls Jo.

After the war, between 1945 and 1951, Landor worked from a small rented office at 556 Commercial Street, on the edge of Chinatown, where, according to Phil Dubrow, a close associate of Landor for decades, "a lot of art teachers had their studios." At the time, the art schools in the Bay area were abuzz with young World War II veterans eager to get an art education. Dubrow remembers Landor telling him that when prospective clients came to visit, Landor would act as if he owned the premises, taking them up and down to meet the various artists in residence. If he got a job—and most of the time, he did—he farmed out the assignments to those ambitious freelancers.

From the start, he thought of himself as a talent broker. Rodney McKnew, who worked with Landor from 1947 to 1988, credits his boss's early successes to what he calls his peripheral vision. "His eye wasn't on the center that held everyone's attention, but off to the side where something far more interesting was happening." Adds Susan Landor: "My father was a master of encounters and meetings. He would sit with the clients and the designers and say nothing at first, listening to everyone until he figured out the politics, the tensions, the possibilities. He only spoke when he had a clear take on the situation."

In 1951, Landor moved his operation to Bush Street, and in

1956, to a small waterfront building on Pier Five. Photographs taken at the time show staff members at lunchtime, basking on a deck overlooking the water, the women in pretty dresses and sunglasses, the men in shirtsleeves holding fishing rods. "Walter's strategy was to create business by having a good time," says Phil Dubrow, who joined the company in 1972, when the relaxed atmosphere was still the trademark of the Landor working environment. "Around the office, there were always eclectic young people and attractive girls with names like Wendy Darling or Nancy Love. They were part of Walter's cheerful entourage. You would bump into them on the decks, taking in the sun. Clients loved it!"

The move to larger quarters gave Landor a chance to focus his professional practice and establish package design as his main specialty. He installed on the premises a mock-up retail environment to help designers and clients visualize the new packages in the real-life context of grocery shelves. "Back in the early days," explains Mim Ryan, "designers did not try to understand consumers or get feedback from them. In the 1960s, eye-tracking and two-way mirrors were new to the marketing field." Hired in 1963 as a research analyst, she helped develop focus groups by creating a full-blown research department, including a large in-house supermarket, complete with two crowded aisles and a freezer case.

In 1964, Landor put a final touch on his brand image by buying an old ferryboat, restoring it, and moving his entire office into it. Anchored on Pier Five, *The Klamath*, as the boat was called, became his proud flagship. It was large enough to accommodate four design departments, a research area for focus groups, a new and improved supermarket environment, a photo studio, and a slide library. But just as important, the boat became the setting of weekly Friday-night floating extravaganzas. Often organized to entertain clients, but just as often to keep the spirit of the place upbeat, the festive events attracted every celebrity who happened to be in San Francisco that night.

As soon as the word was out that Tom Wolfe, Andy Warhol, Howard Gossage, the Grateful Dead, or Marshall McLuhan were expected, 200 of Landor's friends, clients, and protégés would show up to meet the impromptu guests of honor.

Landor drew people to him because he was interested in everyone, even critics who didn't necessarily agree with his design philosophy. "Walter wasn't an ego. He didn't need to leave his fingerprint on the work itself," explains Ryan. "He had a great tolerance for other people's eccentricities. He encouraged everyone to forge ahead and explore new ideas. He took the position that the work coming out of his office was a team effort, not a style statement." An amazing salesman and a savvy businessman, Landor insisted design solutions be relevant, not artistic. "He drove you nuts," says Kay Stout, who was hired in 1974. " He made changes at the last minute to increase 'shelves-impact' rather than aesthetics. He elevated design from decoration to communication. He taught me that good design and good marketing can go together—but it's a lot harder."

Called by his critics "the guy who puts stripes on everything," Landor could layer colors over colors, cartouches over cartouches, and stripes over stripes like no one else. Unlike his contemporaries—Raymond Loewy, Walter Margolies, George Nelson, Saul Bass, and Paul Rand—he didn't have a "house" style. What he had, though, was an uncanny instinct for second-guessing what would appeal to consumers in any given situation. "His approach was humanistic," says John Diefenbach, who went to work for Landor in 1973 as director of client services, and ended up running the company in 1984. "Walter was not in love with the Swiss International Style. He preferred warm, colorful designs. He knew what worked. He understood the appetite appeal of a product. After years of focus groups and consumer feedback, his taste was in perfect sync with that of the public at large."

Landor was a maestro. The last to come into a room (he liked to make an entrance by being a little late), he even looked like a conductor. But with everyone depending on his direction, his comments, and his approval, a lot of time was spent anticipating his next appearance. So much so, in fact, that someone suggested the accounting department issue a job number for "Waiting for Walter."

His loose managerial style, which would eventually be his undoing, was a formidable strength during the first four decades of the company's growth. Landor consistently attracted the best people in the business by creating serendipitous conditions in which everyone had a chance to work on the most interesting projects. "He gave young designers and veterans alike the opportunity to do their best work," says Stout. "Right out of school, you sat down and began to design next to someone twice your age."

Marc Gobé, of Desgrippes Gobé in New York, a leading branding firm, was a young upstart designer in San Francisco in the 1970s. For the Art Director's Club, he had organized a show of then-controversial Polish posters. "Walter Landor came to the opening with an entourage of a dozen young people from his office," he recalls. "A recognized authority in the field, he still was interested in what was new and cutting edge. Right there, I decided to emulate him. I promised to myself to always take the time to mentor members of my staff." Michael Carabetta, now with Chronicle Books in San Francisco, used to work for Landor back then. "The first Thursday of the month, rain or shine, Landor made the rounds of the art galleries, taking us along, and gathering more people as we went," he remembers. "He touched many people's lives with his dapper, man-about-town, worldly approach to the design profession."

But the times were already changing. John Diefenbach can almost pinpoint the exact moment when Landor lost his edge, and with it his control over the company he had created. It was at a meeting in the late 1970s, during which a young designer, freshly hired out of Yale, presented a rather clean and slick-looking design solution—something Landor would usually have rejected. "Walter preferred the fuzzy stuff as a rule," explains Diefenbach. Expecting his boss to ask for something more flowery, Diefenbach couldn't believe it when Landor listened to the presentation and made no objections. "He went along with the general consensus that this staid approach was what the client needed. At that moment, the company changed. "Instead of being driven by a perception of what consumers wanted, design decisions were now driven by a perception of what clients wanted. This was a major shift. Landor Associates was now poised for the 1980s—a decade that turned out to be the most profitable era for the company.

For all his youthful enthusiasm, though, Landor was showing his age; the generation gap became more evident. In 1980, Dubrow was surprised to discover, for instance, that the man who had designed countless soft drink cans and corn chips bags for a number of major league clients had no concept of what fast food was all about. "We were running behind schedule and had no time for lunch," he remembers. "Walter wanted to stop at a good restaurant for a proper meal, as was his habit, but I argued that since we were so late, we'd better pull into a McDonald's and get a couple of hamburgers." Confronted with a burger and a Coke with a straw, Landor had no idea how to proceed. When Dubrow explained to him how to drink and eat the stuff, Landor took the packaging apart, and with nothing short of glee, said "Brilliant!"

All those years, Landor had been an astute tactician, "but not a good strategist," says Dubrow. "He had never been a good manager and he didn't work as hard as we did." Rodney McKnew explains that while most business types were morning people, Landor was a night person, "working late, when no one was around, only interrupting himself for parties." Clay Timon remembers that Landor himself would sometimes vanish for two weeks at a time. "Then he would show up in the Paris office before disappearing again on one of his mini-sabbaticals."

Then, there were all those unbillable hours wasted waiting for

Walter to show up. "Before I came to the company," says Diefenbach, "Walter used to propose up to 150 designs of beer bottles or cigarette packs to clients, all finished drawings!" Indeed, Landor seemed to care more about the fun, the designers, and the creative atmosphere than the bottom line. "The first generation of Landor executives were not as good as managers as the second generation," concedes McKnew. "We served Landor well, but we weren't 'suits.' We were emotionally involved. Our intuition was more developed than our proposal-writing skills." In contrast with Landor's old-world charm, Diefenbach, a charismatic man in his own right, was industrious and aggressive. Under his stewardship, the company became a truly international entity. Though it already had offices in Tokyo, Mexico City, and London, it now was expanding to Washington, Chicago, Seattle, Hong Kong, and Paris. Internal reorganization was also initiated, with teams working more independently, and more efficiently. In what many consider an unnecessary blow to Landor's ego, the offices were moved out of *The Klamath* in 1987, to allow Diefenbach to upgrade the infrastructure and refurbish the interiors to reflect the splashy taste of the Reagan years.

To oppose Diefenbach's ambitious drive, Landor would act dense during their discussions, as if he didn't get the point. The tug-of-war between them was painful to watch for employees who were loyal to Landor, but had to admire Diefenbach's unquestionable leadership. "John was bound to run into problems, " says Timon. "You can't take over the role of an icon."

Landor and Diefenbach would come out of meetings with each other looking exhausted. Walter, always the gentleman, was trembling with repressed anger. Diefenbach was cool and determined. Though the older man was still the star, it was clear to everyone that the younger man ran the company. "We had made earning projections, and exceeded our expectations," explains Dubrow. "As a result of some previous financial arrangements, Walter made a lot more money than what was expected, while John was not getting the financial recognition he deserved."

In 1989, Diefenbach, by now president, CEO, and the main shareholder of Landor Associates, spearheaded a move to buy out Walter Landor. Later that same year, the company was sold to Young & Rubicam, and, according to Dubrow, "everyone did just fine." Diefenbach and Landor Associates parted ways. The new owners promised Landor that they would complete the renovations on *The Klamath*, and move the company back in it. But the reconditioning of the boat was indefinitely postponed. It soon became evident that Landor Associates would be permanently headquartered on Front Street—the silhouette of the ferryboat now only a quaint icon next to the company logo.

"Walter Landor's goal was not to make money, but to be surrounded with people who were different," notes Dubrow. Susan Landor agrees: " My father was a shrewd businessman, but he was never greedy. He was not impressed by the fact that everyone in the 1980s made buckets of money. He cared more about the company he had created." On his tombstone, she says, he wanted the following words "I could not have had a better time."

Landor died in 1995 at the age of 81 after a series of strokes, but today his brand is still very much alive. The firm he spent 54 years nurturing remains in good hands. New clients who come to one of the 12 Landor offices are shown pictures of the ferryboat, and told about the man who championed the idea that understanding consumers and getting their feedback was critical to the design process and the branding of products. Apparently, they are even told about "Captain Walter" and the wild parties on the boat. But whether or not this means anything to them is your guess and mine. As the saying goes, you had to be there.

I was there briefly, in the 1980s, living in San Francisco. Walter Landor and his boat were part of the local folklore. One rainy Friday night, a friend of mine invited me on a date to a party aboard *The Klamath*, with the promise that we would go out for a drink after. The boat was rocking and the place was mobbed. In the push, I couldn't find my friend. I didn't bump into anyone I knew and soon became self-conscious. As I was thinking about leaving, an older gent, who had probably noticed my discomfort, came to my rescue. We began to chat, and in the course of the conversation, I asked him how he came to be here. "I am Walter Landor," he said, "I don't know anyone here, and it's too noisy. Let's go out for a drink."

Now, I thought, wait a minute. He was married and I was single, and his reputation as a flirt was as much part of the local lore as his boat and his prestigious clients. But I was young and reckless back then, so I said why not. We sneaked out of the party and he told me to get in my little Mazda and follow him to a bar he knew. A notoriously bad driver, he headed toward the Golden Gate Bridge at the wheel of his classic Mercedes Coupe convertible. With the rain obscuring my windshield, I had trouble keeping up with him. When we crossed into Marin County he boldly took for the hills.

At long last, he pulled in front of what looked like a deserted Irish bar, an unlikely vision in this pristine and bucolic part of the world. Cold, wet, and somewhat peeved, I slunk onto a stool next to him at the bar. We settled down, ordered beers, and resumed our chat. He seemed genuinely interested to hear about my work, my life, my family. He was a great listener, indeed, with the knack for making you feel special. Watching the city twinkle in the distance over his shoulders through the window, I realized that this was one of those moments when life makes sense: You sit in a funky old bar in the rain with a nice little fellow with a bow tie, while down there, by the bay, the party is still going on.

*When good people make difficult choices
Watching three famous designers
debate the issues of text versus context
and individual mandate versus social
responsibility is the closest thing to
watching three beautiful fish caught in
a treacherous nylon net.*

Day One. The first thing I did when I saw the rows of tables laden with posters, books, brochures, cards, annual reports, and magazines was wring my hands. The 1995 American Center for Design's 100 Show had attracted 1,700 entries. It was the jury's task to select the hundred most worthy of award. Standing next to me, Rudi VanderLans, the founder of *Emigré* magazine was running nervous fingers through his blond hair. Laurie Haycock Makela, then design director of the Walker Art Center in Minneapolis, took a deep breath and began to fidget with the pleats of her skirt. Stephen Doyle, creative director of New York's Drenttel Doyle Partners smiled cryptically and tightened his grip on his coffee cup. All were stars of the design world, and each brought a different perspective to the formidable task at hand.

Who ever said graphic design was a mental discipline? Faced with a roomful of printed material, our initial reaction was intensely physical. A new palpable awareness made the tip of our fingers tingle. Senses sharpened by the smell of ink and the sight of fibrous paper, we circled the tables like hungry predators. Visual curiosity is fed by a delicious tactile craving.

Outside, through the cafeteria bay windows, the kaleidoscopic skyline of Chicago reflected an ever-changing midwestern sky. Inside, the landscape was just as variegated. Acre upon acre of prime intellectual real estate in the form of contest submissions reflected the multifaceted concerns of untold numbers of people, institutions, and businesses.

The rules of the game are simple, we are told. The three judges are independent of each other and can proceed as they want. The first day they are only required to select entries they wish to consider. With colored Post-It notes, they save worthy submissions from being unceremoniously dismissed. The second day they will be invited to edit their selection. A civilized process, the system is designed to foster a sense of nonconformity. This is the land of the free—and the brave.

At first, the three judges hesitate at the edge of this graphic

wilderness. They huddle together in the annual reports and corporate brochures area. "Can we peek at the names of the designers?" asks Laurie. "Can we talk to each other?" asks Stephen.
"Is there money under the entries?" inquires Rudi.

Urged to do as they please, they each go their own way. For
a while you only hear the dry flutter of pages, the occasional
flapping of a soft cover and the furtive pat of a hand on a piece
of paper. Expressive textures combined with a deliberate economy of images give this show an irresistible sensuality. The two-
dimensional surface is striving to acquire a three-dimensional
status. Intricate annual reports masquerade as old-fashioned fil-
ing systems. Catalogues are designed to look like unedited man-
uscripts. You don't simply open a brochure anymore—you peel,
unfurl, take apart, and unwrap. Gaining access to the written
material can be quite a project.

"If you can't figure out what it is," asks Rudi, "is it good or
bad?" He is holding in his hand a Chicago Volunteer Legal
Services piece that looks like a cross between an accounting
ledger and a quaint dog-eared file folder. "It's weird—but
maybe it has fantastic content," he adds. Oblivious of the
remaining 1,684 entries, he pulls up a red plastic chair, sits down
comfortably and proceeds to read the brochure cover to cover.

Good design can be conducive to bad behavior. While Rudi
stubbornly deconstructs the Chicago Volunteer Legal Service
brochure, Stephen inspects a local eatery's lunch menu. "It's an
electronic macramé of typographical errors," he comments. "No
production value—but delightfully under-designed. I wonder if
I should order the roasted chicken salad sandwich." Laurie
decides to forge ahead—and makes a beeline for the literary
journals displayed in the next room. "I have a low tolerance for
self-promotion pieces," she remarks, bypassing 20 tables
jammed-packed with Christmas cards and invitations mixed
together with corporate identity program entries. "I'll look at
that area after lunch."

Progress is slow—as soon as a table is "judged," it is cleared and fresh new entries are immediately laid out. A Sisyphean labor indeed. But the serenity of the support staff is unfaltering. Taking unhurried notes is the chair of the show, the unflappable Rick Poynor, founder of the London-based *Eye Magazine*. Rob Dewey, the Art Director's Club (ADC) director of communications, operates ominously from backstage. The official fly on the wall, I apologize each time I bump into someone. Because of the enormity of the task, everyone acts very cool.

Yet something is definitely amiss. The work submitted cannot be judged at leisure in these conditions. It would take months for a team of experts to give each entry the kind of attention it richly deserves. I check on Rudi, who seems to have given up on the Chicago Volunteer Legal Services brochure and is now engrossed in a portfolio, a sedate catalogue of Italian watercolors for the Krannert Art Museum. "Who is this artist Al Held?" he asks me. "Is he important? I like the design of the brochure but I don't like his work very much. Does it matter? What's relevant here?" Stephen, overhearing our conversation, answers without missing a beat: "The only relevant question to ask ourselves is: Do we want next year's annual reports to look like this?"

Suddenly it occurs to me that the outcome of the weekend will not be the objective selection of the 100 best entries—scrap that idea—but the collective reaffirmation of our commitment to design as a noble and worthy discipline. The judging process is a ritualistic event during which the judges—not the entries—are coming under scrutiny. The mandate of Rudi, Laurie, and Stephen is to define who we are by reaching for universal predicaments concealed under narrative pieces. In order to do the job, the judges must put their idiosyncrasies aside, personify their point of view, and accept being typecast. The transformation takes place in less than two hours. By 11:00 A.M., Stephen is assuming the role of the corporate type; Rudi impersonates the *artiste*; Laurie has embraced the part of the new woman.

Dapper Stephen—in Lee jeans, J. Crew polo shirt worn over

a white cotton tee, half-deckers, and croco belt—is the one who always gets it first. While you are still trying to figure out how to open the brochure, he already has a handle on what it all means. "I wonder how their business is doing," he remarks dryly in front of an overproduced corporate brochure. A slick paper promotion has him wondering if we invent simple-minded problems in order to come up with astute design solutions. He has the gift of the gab. "Scribbles, circumcised typography..." he mutters when inspecting a self-indulgent digitized graphic exercise. His choices tend to be bookish, handsome, and culturally meaningful. He is the Charlie Rose of our profession.

Rudi, who wears his Levi's Euro-style with an olive green twill shirt untucked, white socks, and black shoes, makes a point of never taking anything for granted. "I don't know what this is," he says repeatedly. "Are we judging a beauty pageant?" he asks later in all earnestness. And then, faced with yet another example of how not to use Template Gothic, one of his popular *Emigré* typefaces, he quips: "It's funny, I should be happy to see how many people use my products, but all I can think is did they pay for it?" A champion of the playful and the unformatted, he is endlessly fascinated by under-produced, monochromatic conceptual pieces.

Laurie, who stashes her Post-It notes in her bra to keep her hands free, wears a short pleated skirt, a Jeff Koons T-shirt tucked-in, black hose, and no shoes. Caring and curious, she wants to know how all these posters, catalogues, reports, T-shirts, and invitations have performed for the people they were destined for. "How did it affect the collective energy?" she wonders aloud. "It's too decorative—but maybe that's part of the reason it works," she says of a museum calendar. She is the one who notices that most female names on entry slips identify the "entrant"—the person who mailed the competition—not the "designer"—who will get credit for it. A discussion ensues. Who is Sarah Haun, Pentagram's "entrant"? Jenna Maliza, with Frankfurt Gips Balkind? Sally Howe, who filled so many slips for Jager DiPaola Kemp? Anne Dolan, employed by Duffy Design? For Laurie, no matter what people do, if they are involved, they become an integral part of the process. "These entries reflect a collective mind," she says, "not the intention of a few individuals."

By mid-afternoon, the judges, now working in sync, have weeded through more than a thousand projects. Stephen's blue stickers are few and far between. Laurie's green ones earmark community and institutional projects. Rudi's pink slips are everywhere—the editor-in-chief of *Emigré* has adopted a liberal nonrestrictive policy.

In spite of the apparent randomness of the process, trends are emerging. Tribalism, recognizable by its wild electronic typography and full-bodied color palette, is on the rise—but David Carson has peaked. The snow-boarding industry is still on the leading edge of graphic innovations. Waste management companies make the best clients. Handwriting is still in favor. Honesty and self-parody are critical design ingredients. Education has replaced information—a "show, don't tell" approach is making a big comeback.

Day Two. This morning Rudi wears a white T-shirt; Stephen sports a yellow striped shirt; Laurie has donned a Walker Center T-shirt with tightly rolled short sleeves. Apostles of the new design testament, they are ready for their ultimate test—the editing down of yesterday's freewheeling selection. Each judge is allowed about 35 submissions. For Stephen and Laurie, this means refining their philosophy. For Rudi, it's a daunting task. He looks pale and confides that he didn't sleep last night. "I don't know that I can do the job," he says.

First comes the exegesis—the exposition—an attempt by our three judges to create a critical context from which to proceed. Stephen sits down on the edge of a chair, Laurie leans back on a table, and Rudi hunkers down, one knee on the floor. The discussion centers around the relevance of the judging process, a phase Rob Dewey views from a distance with a touch of apprehension. All juries, he knows from experience, must sooner or later pass through this painful stage in order to come to terms with their final selection.

Watching them debate the issues of text versus context and individual mandate versus social responsibility is the closest thing to watching three beautiful fish caught in a treacherous nylon net. Poynor looks away. Volunteering students, who have gathered around the group to listen, stare at their shoes. Curiosity incites me to join in the debate—and it's not long before I regret it. No one can alleviate the discomfort that precedes a moment of truth.

The pressure to do the right thing is such that soon the judging process resumes and moves swiftly toward its preordained conclusion. This is a design competition—good taste must prevail in the end.

Nonetheless, the Seventh Annual 100 Show is prone to quirkiness. Laurie, Stephen, and Rudi are now engaged in tough ethical negotiations intended to protect individual voices, promote relevance, and define quality. Collaborative efforts between writers and designers are rewarded; nonelitist projects are favored; weird, homespun, and obsessive pieces benefit from a little extra consideration. Chuck Anderson's work is viewed as eccentric. A politically incorrect Mohawk project is severely reprimanded. Visual statements using every trick in the book make no good impression.

After Rudi peels off 36 pink Post-It notes from his original pile of selected entries, the Chicago Volunteer Legal Services brochure is still in the running. A student project, *Margo Johnston's Hybrid Digital Typeface Book*, wins everybody's vote. A stamp of approval is given to Coca-Cola's gimmicky Generation X "OK" can. Clement Mok's CD library of clip art is adopted unanimously. Each of these finalists is clever, graphically arresting, and has a certain level of complexity.

But the big surprise of the show is how good the judges feel about the most unlikely project, one that does not fit in any category: a handrail for the blind, with directions in Braille tucked out of sight under a slim oak banister. It's the final revenge: the most clearly defined entry features design you can't see but can only touch. An entire weekend spent groping in the dark for valid design standards is redeemed by a single invisible tactile stroke. It makes perfect sense: After all, we're here to provide direction. Like the blind, designers need guidelines in order to find their way around. Each selected piece in the 100 Show is but a raised dot on the seamless surface of our professional practice. Decipher this Braille message, and you'll know where to find the exit door. Competitions are meant to help you look ahead, not over your shoulder.

Before leaving, the judges shake hands. That contact neutralizes the spell. Rudi wanders out; Laurie rushes to the phone to find out how her child is doing; Stephen gets to make one last comment: "We always want to push design forward," he says, "but we never ask forward where?" We laugh and each make our own exits—back to New York, Minneapolis, San Francisco, London.

The merchandising of facts
At the 1964 World's Fair in New York,
everyone assumed that smart robots, picturephones, and household computers were a
done deal. Words like *knowledge, discovery,*
and understanding were the rage.

I t was my first job ever in America. The assigment: design a 12-foot-long plywood replica of a malignant cell.

"It should look like something from outer space," explained my boss.

For a second or two, I was dumbfounded. Up until this moment, design for me had been synonymous with form and function, harmony and beauty. Perhaps I had misunderstood.

"Do you want me to make the cancer look streamlined?" I asked in my faltering English.

"Keep it realistic," he said. "We will light it from behind to make it glow." The giant protoplasm was to be part of an exhibit for the American Cancer Society in the Hall of Science at the 1964–65 New York World's Fair.

On a one-semester break from the Beaux-Arts architecture school in Paris, I was in New York on a student visa. I had landed a position in the exhibit design department of the prestigious firm of Loewy/Snaith where Raymond Loewy—famous for designing the torpedo-shaped Pennsylvania Rail Road steam engine, the aerodynamic Studebaker, and the streamlined Frigidaire—was still running the show.

Alright. I didn't expect to be asked to design another Rocketport—a supersonic sci-fi launch pad like the one Loewy had created for the Chrysler pavilion at the previous New York World's Fair in 1939. But I was hoping for something modernistic, like a bus stop perhaps, or a drinking fountain. An oversized cancer cell? For crying out loud, I was an architecture student, not an expert in exfoliative cytology.

Live and learn. In the next 14 years as an exhibit designer, I worked on displays, dioramas, and multimedia presentations covering a wide range of subjects, from the nesting habits of penguins to the health advantages of barbecuing. I now know that trivia is where it's at. Furthermore, you don't have to be an expert to be a good visual communicator. The truth be told, it's better if you are clueless. I grew to love edifying people about things I knew nothing about—so much so in fact that I eventually became a journalist.

This was my first encounter with a discipline that was still in its infancy but has since become big business: the merchandising of facts—what retail guru Leslie Wexner, CEO of the Limited Inc., calls "information as entertainment." For the next few months, I labored over a number of graphic displays dramatizing uterine cancer and the life-saving wonders of the Pap test. The exhibit's main objective was to encourage women visitors to ask their doctors for routine annual uterine cancer checkups.

Although the communications technology was still rudimentary at best in the early 1960s, in the public's imagination it was already perfected. As far as people were concerned, smart robots, picturephones, and household computers were a done deal. Words like *knowledge*, *discovery*, and *understanding* were the rage. The main theme of the 1964 New York World's Fair, "Peace Through Understanding," was indicative of this new passion for communication.

At the fair, visitors were treated to countless live demonstrations, interactive exhibits, show-and-tells, animated displays, documentary movies, instructive slide presentations, and educational rides. There was more raw data per capita than at any previous international exhibition or world's fair. In eclectic pavilions thrown pell-mell around the 12-story-high stainless-steel Unisphere, a total of 80 countries, 24 states, and 200 companies spun their tale of success for 50 million visitors over the two consecutive seasons. It was the biggest and most well-attended object lesson to date.

While national and regional pavilions preferred the linear approach to storytelling—retracing their history with films, demonstrations, and displays of handicrafts—American corporations spared no expense to entertain fun-seeking fairgoers with memorable "experiences" in order to get their message across. Clairol offered a complete hair-coloring analysis during a six-minute glass-enclosed carousel ride; in a gleaming gold disk floating 24 feet above ground, Johnson's Wax gave free shoe shines; Parker Pen, with the help of a primitive computer, matched visitors with compatible pen pals around the world; Simmons told the story of sleep from rock to pillow—and provided carpeted rest alcoves where, for a dollar, tired visitors could take 30-minute restorative naps.

At 11 strategic locations throughout the fair, General Foods, in collaboration with Time/Life, installed "Archways to Understanding," horseshoe towers that delivered "a constant flow of facts about happenings on and off the fairgrounds." Under the Travelers Insurance Red Umbrella pavilion, an electronic display recorded every birth and death in the country, almost as fast as they occurred. At the Westinghouse pavilion, a time capsule was suspended high above a reflecting pool. It contained information intended to help people 5,000 years from now understand our culture. Among the artifacts were a Polaroid camera, a bikini, an electric toothbrush, birth control pills, credit cards, and microfilm with 117,000 pages of written and pictorial information.

But by far the most talked-about experience at the fair was a ride up inside the IBM "information machine," a multiscreen theater enclosed in an egg-shaped dome. There, a short film, produced by Charles and Ray Eames, explained the similarities between computers and the human brain. Lively sequences showed how a woman's mind works when she plans the seating at a dinner party, how scientists break down complex problems, and how race car drivers make split-second decisions on the track. "See how computers use your own everyday way of reasoning to solve some of the universe's most mystifying riddles," implored the IBM informational leaflet.

I was there on the fair's opening day, eager to check on my oversized protoplasm. As I crossed the fairgrounds toward the Hall of Science (housed next to the U.S. Space Park where "the largest array of spacecrafts outside Cape Kennedy was displayed"), I felt no peace through understanding—only a mounting sense of anxiety. The fair was the ugliest architectural sprawl I had ever seen. Unlike the 1939–40 fair, it lacked the sponsorship of the Bureau of International Expositions. Aptly nicknamed the "laissez-fair" by critics, it offered the first glimpse of a future no one was prepared to deal with: one in which the individual would progressively lose control over the flow of information.

Subsequently, I worked on the Montreal Expo 67, on the 1970 World Exposition in Osaka, and on a number of highly forgettable trade shows, exhibits, and displays. I also got married, had a child, got divorced, and all along struggled to keep up with my colleagues in the field—with what Robert Moses, the 1964 World's Fair president had described as "the Olympics of Progress." I felt I wasn't getting anywhere until one day I got a big break: Milton Glaser asked me to join his team to collaborate with architect I.M. Pei and French film archivist Henri Langlois. The project was exciting: to create an American museum of cinema under New York's 59th Street Bridge. At long last, I would work on a prestigious cultural landmark.

At our first briefing, we discussed location, budget, square footage, and schedules. Langlois had not yet arrived from Paris, so no one knew for sure what sort of artifacts would be on display. A substantial part of the budget was allocated for acquisitions, but there was no plan yet to hire a curator. Did we have a concept, I asked? That's why you are here, I was told. Give us some ideas. You are an exhibit designer, aren't you?

I went home and began to draw. In my mind's eye, I saw a series of smoke screens on which Hollywood classics would be projected. Visitors would travel on ski lifts through this maze of ethereal moving images; here, they would glide through Marilyn Monroe's lips; there, they would zoom on Dustin Hoffman's face in the last scene of *The Graduate*. I tried to pull every trick of the trade: I proposed a giant soft sculpture of a popcorn kernel for the lobby, a paparazzi tunnel where visitors would be blinded by flashes, a Casablanca café, a full-scale replica of the

Singin' in the Rain fountain. It was going to be fun—a post-modern version of the celluloid experience.

Who was I kidding? Sure, I had plenty of ideas and no short-age of imagination—but in earnest, I had nothing to say. Eagerness to design cannot replace a point of view. No amount of creativity can be a substitute for true investigation. Too often in our business we try to bypass the labor-intensive research phase and go straight to the design solutions. In doing so, we miss a chance to come across some unexpected insight. In the previous decade, working under time pressure, I had been asked over and over to come up with visually striking yet empty con-cepts. Not once did I feel that my job was to enlighten viewers strolling through the exhibition.

So I put down my pencil. I knew at once that I had come to the end of my career as an exhibit designer. I had gimmicks, but no ideas behind them. I'll never forget the look of irritation on Milton Glaser's face when I told him I was resigning because I had nothing to bring to the project. Ever since, the memory of my utter embarrassment has kept me from throwing one more mediocre idea on paper.

Is design an art or a craft?
The truth is, whether still struggling or
manifestly successful, designers are always
marginalized. First by clients, who want all
the credit for the innovations. Then by the
public, who believes that designers are
folks who put their names on jeans.

I n a crowd, I can always spot fellow designers who are like me: opinionated, restless, eclectic—and the product of a slapdash undergraduate art education. In this business, if you never thumbed through *The Technique of the Observer* by Jonathan Crary, somehow, it shows. You can't fool me. Something in your body language tells me that you break into hives at the mere mention of Roland Barthes and that you never had to spell Hochschule für Gestaltung.

I too used to snub the work of Jonathan Crary, John Berger, Edward Tufte, Ellen Lupton, and J. Abbot Miller.

Worse, I used to pooh-pooh the Aspen Design Conference and the MoMA crowd; I had to be sedated to look through design annuals; and I assumed that Jacques Derrida was a famous French chef. Watch me now. I am a born-again intellectual, an AIGA card–carrying member, and an *Emigré* magazine groupie. But deep inside, I am still a loner. I define design on my own terms: I've become a writer.

What happened? I realized that trying to ignore the intellectual concerns of my peers was just as ludicrous as trying to ignore the new technology. Although, from time to time, unschooled designers do burst on the scene fully realized (no, not David Carson; he paid his dues like everyone else), most of us can no longer afford to lock ourselves in our studios. Design is not about providing form anymore, it's about "contextualization." But you knew that, of course.

British design critic Rick Poynor commiserates with designers who used to derive great intellectual pleasure from the exercise of their craft—but who are now expected to be intellectual theorists. "What's happening today is unfair to designers," Poynor says. "They are told that reading and readability are old-fashioned concerns—yet, at the same time, they are supposed to read long speculative texts by French philosophers that no one, frankly, can read, let alone understand." If you haven't been trained at Cranbrook, RISD, CalArts, Yale, Ulm, Basel, or the like, all this fuss about post-structuralism and semiotics can get on your nerves. To paraphrase Paula Scher, sometimes it feels like design-speak was created to give credence to a profession encumbered with a commercial-art inferiority complex.

In 1997, at the AIGA design conference in New Orleans, I sat down with 2,500 other design professionals who, like me, had fastened their mental seatbelt to listen to a wide range of new and challenging theories, constructs, and ideas that pertain to our field. The Clutter of Images and The Disorder of Sequence. The Tangible Touch. The Politics of Performance. The Corridor of Possibilities. The Sensual vs. The Intellectual. As the various speakers delivered their lectures on the main stage, you could feel the static in the room as neurons fired in all directions.

But you could also feel the old, anti-intellectual resistance building up all around. Restlessness. Whispers. Some grumbling. Rummaging through shopping bags full of tantalizing promotional freebies and lavish paper samples from generous conference sponsors. "I'll skip the next presentation and go for the free T-shirts," said a loud male voice behind me.

Free T-shirts? Touché. The gentleman was obviously an enlightened skeptic, someone endowed with a sense of humor—and a low threshold for contextualization. Not bashful about letting everyone know that he had had enough of the "Jambalaya" of cool pronouncements and mind-expanding observations the AIGA had cooked up for him, he packed up noisily and left. In the middle of the theater, his empty seat marked the center of some ominous sinkhole. Could it be that our profession is about to be sucked into abstraction? Remember: We treasure design as a means to make the invisible visible—not the other way around.

Too bad he left, though. He would have agreed with the next speaker, designer-educator Lorraine Wild, who explored the reason why "design" transcends mere design solutions. "The meaning of our work is based on how things are done, not conceptualized," she offered. "Let's not undervalue the pleasure and knowledge of the craft." Earlier, designer Stephen Doyle had expressed a similar sentiment. "As designers, we think with our hands. Things with fingerprints on them are so darn reassuring. The tactile experience is crucial to our business."

Interestingly enough, Wild and Doyle were the only two designers invited to discourse on the main stage. The other key speakers were filmmakers, architects, journalists, art historians, performance artists, jazzmen, and cyber jockeys. The star moderator, John Hockenberry, an NBC television news commentator whose penetrating remarks alone were worth the price of admission, had never been in a design studio.

For the audience, all this brilliant insight from nonprofessionals was a subtle put-down. The truth is, whether still struggling or manifestly successful, designers are always marginalized. First by clients, who want all the credit for the innovations. Then by the public, who believes that designers are folks who put their names on jeans. And last but not least by the art world, which figures designers are artists who can't take the heat.

In his opening remarks at the New Orleans design conference, Richard Grefé, AIGA's executive director, had tried to caution the audience. "Don't expect us to define graphic design," he'd said. "Whatever it is, it's not about graphic design per se; it's about creativity and inspiration." Forewarned is forearmed. Even within our profession, we are not quite sure that graphic design is a topic worthy of discussion.

About half a million individuals are currently practicing graphic design in America, yet only a small percentage ever bothered to find out what their profession was all about by going to school. Hair colorists need a license to practice their craft, but we don't. To this day, the U.S. Department of Labor classifies graphic design as a trade that doesn't require college study. And the software industry encourages prospective designers to think that software literacy—a skill that can be acquired in one session—is more or less equivalent to a four-year design degree.

Still, according to a white paper sponsored by the AIGA,

about 10,000 design students enroll every year in art schools. There are more than 2,000 graphic design programs for them to choose from around the country—each with a different curriculum. These art schools have responded to the growing demand for design education by staffing newly minted communication departments with underqualified teachers—mostly studio artists with little professional experience who consider design a subset of fine art. Many of their students are far more computer literate than they are. Adding insult to injury, these ill-conceived graphic design programs are the cash cows that finance the poorly attended fine art classes. No wonder design students who attend these academic establishments end up with educational gaps that leave them forever handicapped.

"Design has no subject matter of its own," says Poynor, echoing Grefé's remark. "It's a complex act of control at the crossroads of art and commerce, linguistics and logic, anthropology and art history, just to name a few. Most schools cannot teach this discipline because they are too busy legitimizing the students' reluctance to get involved with words." A design critic, Poynor is an ink-based wordsmith. He is nostalgic for the days when designers and writers shared the same passion for typographical clarity and precision. "Most conferences, in the States as well as Europe, try to fill the vacuum left by design education by offering word-intensive presentations—expecting attendees to synthesize the content. But it's a lot to ask of anyone. Frankly, I believe that the whole discussion would be better on paper. That's why you have books and magazines—to allow time for reflection."

Could it be that design, like philosophy, is a mental discipline rather than a craft—a specialty that should not be taught as a marketable skill? "Do we really have anything to offer apart from the sometimes questionable promise of a job?" asks Gunnar Swanson, head of the graphic design program at the University of Minnesota Duluth. "Philosophy teachers do not measure success based on whether the majority of their students become philosophers." Likewise, why measure the success of our design education based on our professional activity? After all, adds Swanson, everyone agrees that graphic design students would benefit from studying anthropology, but would anthropology students benefit from the study of graphic design?

The answer, of course, is "yes." In antiquity, architecture and philosophy were considered one and the same discipline. An appreciation of beauty was a prerequisite for understanding logic, ethics, and mathematics. In my own experience, I credit the 30 years I spent as a practicing designer for my more recent achievements as a writer. After all, I learned to craft words by studying work by the likes of Paul Rand, Bradbury Thompson, Saul Bass, Massimo Vignelli, Robert Venturi, Paula Scher, and Rudi VanderLans.

Space for real intimacy
Dressing in the morning is still, for most
of us, a form of meditation. When asked
to describe their grooming and dressing
routines, people will cheerfully comply and
talk about the most minute details
with great precision.

Taking a shower, in the land of the free, is an equal opportunity ritual: it turns ordinary citizens into crowned heads. We, the people, start the day naked but regal, proudly wearing a diadem of water.

Unfortunately, in America, as soon as you step out of the shower stall, you lose your princely status. Turn off the water, and the bathroom becomes a grim and slippery cell. The decor is spartan and bleak: the tiles are usually ugly, the furnishings are minimal. European bathrooms, in contrast, are real rooms, often with a window and enough space for a small table and a couple of side chairs. They encourage people to linger and dally in the nude, take their time, and, if they feel like it, read a couple of pages from a book.

That's not all. Abroad, most traditional apartments include a spare room that serves as a dressing room for the entire family. It is usually carpeted and lined with floor-to-ceiling closets. There is enough space for a large mirror, an open ironing board, a freestanding clothes rack, a couple of chests, and a small washbasin tucked behind sliding doors. It is the room where you dress and undress, but also where you lock yourself up with your sister to talk about boys and where you hide to have a good cry. There, you find Christmas wrapping paper, the embroidery kit bought five years ago in Germany, and the chair with the broken leg. A haven for anyone in need of privacy, it combines the mystery of an attic, the fresh and fragrant atmosphere of a laundry room, and the secretive intimacy of a boudoir.

There is no such thing in America. As you tiptoe out of the steamed-up bathroom wrapped in a towel, you will not find a friendly spot to rest your bare bottom. You have to keep moving, like someone on the run. There is a furtive quality to the dressing process. Putting your clothes on is carried out like a clandestine operation; you ransack your drawers, looking for your underwear; you pilfer your closet, hoping to find something to wear; you leap on one foot, while putting on your hose or your socks; the place soon looks a mess. Getting dressed in

America is the most uncivilized act of the day.

Yet, to look good, one has to dress right. A rigorous methodology is the only way to keep track of the all-important grooming details. Louis XIV, who practically invented the concept of
fashion, created for himself the most elaborate dressing ritual.
Seven days a week for the 33 years of his reign, he observed the
same wake-up ceremonial. The *Grand Lever*, as the royal *toilette*
was called, was an orchestrated affair—with the king's bedroom
designed like a stage to accommodate it. The monarch remained
stationary, sitting in his armchair, while the supporting cast, featuring doctors, valets, butlers, attendants, family members, visiting dignitaries, and special guests, followed a rigid script. The
grand chamberlain's function was to remove the king's night-
cap. A prince of royal blood brought him his shirt. The first
valet introduced His Majesty's barber, who would then instruct
his assistant to give the king a shave. Even the props (tables,
chairs, basins, wigs, robes, brushes, and other grooming implements) were brought in and out following a tedious and repetitive ballet.

The ceremony itself cannot be credited for the success of the
royal regime, but the court's commitment to it was so impressive
that no one dared to question the absolute authority of its creator. The next sovereigns, Louis XV and Louis XVI, tried to
keep the court rituals, but slowly lost interest in them. By the
time the Bastille fell, and with it the French monarchy, the king
had become so lazy that he seldom bothered to wear his wigs.

No one today would care to duplicate the setup of the *Grand
Lever*. Who wants to be treated like a patient? Even if you could
afford it, you wouldn't welcome people trudging back and forth
in your bedroom, passing the instruments as in a surgical pro-
cedure. Our concept of intimacy has evolved since the time of
Louis XIV. The body is now private, and everything that touch-
es it is personal. While dressing and undressing, we proceed
according to patterns that are designed to eliminate intimate
details. We use screens, doors, curtains. Our clothes are also kept

hidden in closets, drawers, and boxes. But with so much kept out of sight, no one knows anymore how to manage the transition between our private and public self—no one knows anymore how to dress. We learn from movies how to take our clothes off, but not how to put them on. In films, scenes showing actors dressing in the morning are usually reserved for bedroom comedies. Pulling up one's pants is the stuff of slapstick.

Creating space for real intimacy is seldom a concern of architects who are pressured by their clients to design houses and apartments with the camera angle in mind—a living room or a bedroom being first and foremost potential spreads in magazines. No one wants to publish a house with a lot of dead space, empty hallways, bare corners. As a result, there is no mystery, no hiding place, no spare room in modern dwellings. Every square inch is exploited for maximum drama. There is very little "in-between" space. You can't even stop and think—keep moving, you are in the way.

"I keep my electric razor in the umbrella stand," says a friend who moved into a new apartment, "because it is the only place where the plug and the mirror are in the right position." He is considering growing a beard. In most rental units, the only open space where you can dress comfortably is usually in front of a window. Custom-designed interiors can be just as unpractical: "I try to stay out of my bedroom; it looks so much better when I am not in it," confesses a woman whose apartment was published in a chic magazine. "In the morning, I take all my clothes out, and dress in the dining room."

With the exception of the Shakers, few American designers have been inspired by household *objets* relating to storage. Today, it's not unusual for an architect to bemoan the fact that he was commissioned to add $500,000 worth of closet, dressing, and storage space to an existing house, one originally designed by him. One might as well bemoan man's fall from grace. When God chased Adam and Eve from the Garden of Eden and told them to cover their shame, He created clothing—along with clutter. Hatboxes. Ironing boards. Hampers. Plastic garment bags. These everyday items will forever be subtle reminders of our original sin.

Perhaps that's why dressing in the morning is still, for most of us, a form of meditation. When asked to describe their grooming and dressing routine, people will cheerfully comply and talk about the most minute details with great seriousness. Whether they take a shower before or after breakfast; at what point in the process they feed the cat or walk the dog; how often they look in the mirror; where they keep their shoes, their keys, their glasses. These careful narratives are precious records of some of the most meaningful moments of the day, a time during which we accomplish a double task: protect our private self while asserting our public identity—become more human, yet less vulnerable.

Louis XIV built a majestic chapel next to his royal bedroom. All I'm asking for is a little dressing room.

Art Kane: an eye for glamour
His obituary in The New York Times
identified him as the photographer
of the "Great Day in Harlem" picture.
But that was only one of his
thousand-word images.

In 1965, Art Kane took a memorable photograph of a little black girl hugging a white doll. Brutal in its simplicity, the picture was published in a *Look* magazine photo essay, and became one of the most bittersweet symbols of the Civil Rights movement. Twenty-two years later, I was art directing *Parenting* magazine and needed an illustration for a piece on racism. I wanted to update the photograph, but I was nervous. Asking Art Kane to repeat himself was like asking George and Ira Gershwin to rewrite "Our Love Is Here to Stay." But when I called Kane and asked him if he would consider reshooting the image as a cover, to my surprise, he said yes.

Tall, handsome, and still youthful looking at 62, Art Kane was a legendary New York artist, a photographer with the charisma of a movie star. And indeed, like a star, he always had an entourage—assistants, stylists, reps, hair and makeup artists, casting agents, gofers, and prop people. To take one picture, he hired a small crowd. And the *Parenting* cover was no exception. Soon, I found myself quibbling with an army of strangers about the choice of model, her outfit, her pigtails, and whether or not we should pluck her eyebrows and remove her tiny gold earrings. Then I watched in disbelief as the hair stylist gave the doll a chic haircut.

But who was I to object? Kane was one of few photographers who could create an artificial setup for a photograph and make it look believable. Preparation was key. "My greatest joy in the whole medium is conceiving ideas and arranging all the preliminaries that go into the picture," he said once. Image-making, more than picture-taking, was his business.

Born Arthur Kanosky in the Bronx in 1925, Kane had been a successful photographer for three decades. He'd become famous for his interpretative portraits of rock stars, artists, celebrities and models. In the fifties, he was known as a young and fearless editorial designer, first at *Esquire* and then at *Seventeen* magazine, where his layouts won numerous awards. At age 27, he was the youngest art director of a major magazine, hiring some of the best photographers of his days, including Bert Stern, Richard Avedon, and Francesco Scavullo. In 1958, he switched careers to become a photographer, but kept his art director mentality. He was always searching for ways to communicate ideas rather than simply take pictures. Some art directors loved to let him take the lead—Allen Hurlburt at *Look* and Robert Benton at *Esquire*—but others resented his dictatorial vision. "My dad didn't speak much about the art directors he worked with," remembers Jonathan Kane, who used to assist his father on shoots during school breaks. "He was The Art Director himself. In many instances, it wasn't a happy relationship. He never listened to them. So they would be frustrated, steal into a corner, not knowing what to do with themselves."

I, too, was hushed out of the way. Forced inaction gave me plenty of time to watch Kane and see how he was going to pull off the image a second time around. Duplicating an icon isn't easy, particularly one with a political message. In 1971, photojournalist Eugene Richards had done just that. On assignment in Arkansas, he had reinvented that very same image. He snapped the picture of a black girl holding a white doll's head to her face, as if it were a mask. Published in *Life* magazine, Richards' disturbing photograph was almost frightening whereas Kane's original image was simply poignant. "Your total life experience will ultimately pop out [in your pictures], one way or another," Kane once said. I was curious to find out how his life experience—what he had learned during the last two decades—would influence the outcome of the reshoot.

Kane was famous for never leaving anything to chance. He would draw roughs beforehand, test various wide-angle lenses, do research, and hunt around for the right location and the right props. "Art took two weeks to take one picture," says Henry Wolf, who knew him well. The two men had met when Kane was at *Seventeen* and Wolf was art director at *Esquire*. "He went out in the rain, stood on top of ladders, did the real thing." But convinced that reality seldom lives up to its promise, Art Kane didn't leave it at that. He manipulated his slides afterward, often turning images upside down and sandwiching them on top of each other. "Once you have the audacity to extract an image from a living, breathing, totally dimensional world," he said, "you've eliminated smell, touch, sound.... In that sense, no photograph is the truth." The only truth for him was his own experience. "Kane didn't photograph people doing their thing; he photographed them doing his thing," wrote Tom Piazza, in *American Photo*. My first shoot with Kane was a chance for me to observe at leisure how a photographer imprints his own vision on film.

Alone on the set with the model and her plastic doll (when he was shooting, everyone had to hide), Kane stood squarely next to his camera and waited. He didn't particularly enjoy kids, but he understood them. He felt that, like him, they were stubborn and self-centered. He had shot many children in his career. In fact, he was the only photographer of his generation and talent who stooped to look at them through a lens. Since the 1965 *Look* shoot, he had produced and directed a short film on games children play for the U.S. pavilion at the Montreal Expo, taken countless pictures of kids with the American flag, and shot a multicultural tribute to babyhood for Johnson & Johnson. His most provocative baby picture to date was a group portrait of Frank Zappa and The Mothers of Invention cuddling with two dozen naked infants. (At one point all the kids started urinating, Kane recalled. "It was like the fountains of Rome.")

Kane used gentle coercion to get what he wanted from sitters. Robert Benton, who later became a filmmaker, developed his directing technique from watching Kane at shoots. "I learned from him that you don't tell people what to do—you let them do what they are going to do," he explained. Through the cracks, I watched Kane wait until the child was ready to come out; wait for her to shed her good-little-girl behavior; wait for her to be bored. Then, all he did was look at her with his big-white-man eyes. Instinctively, she held onto her doll a little tighter, her body language saying "don't you dare take it away." That's what he had hoped for. A gut reaction; a swagger; the eye contact with someone unafraid to stand her ground. Not a sixties waif but an eighties brat; not an oppressed kid—a confident one. In my 15 years as an art director, it remains my favorite cover.

For Kane, photography was a way of life, not a way to make a living. He only took assignments that gave him a chance to try something new. As soon as clients expected him to do things one way—perhaps repeat a particular wide-angle technique he had perfected—he would come up with something else. "He has probably turned down enough editorial commissions to keep several photographers busy," noted Allen Hurlburt. As if being picky about assignments weren't enough, Kane was also a ruthless editor of his work. "I'll throw away anything that's obvious," he once said. In his studio, remembers his son Jonathan, there were garbage bins full of his own slides. "Other photographers would have killed for the kind of pictures he threw away. Had he not edited his work, his estate would now have 60,000 slides instead of the 10,000 we probably have now."

Always busy and always up to something—on weekends he would move the furniture—Kane never seemed concerned about his financial future. "We all had big budgets back then," says Wolf who, like Kane, switched from art direction to photography. "Until the mid-80s, we never had to worry about fees or expenses. Clients would throw money at us." Even though Kane didn't treat art directors like VIPs, they continued to pay for his extravagant expenses. "And the people were so nice," adds Wolf. "They supported photographers to the tune of millions. You never had to haggle."

Sometime in the eighties, as old-timers can attest, things changed. According to Wolf, it was imperceptible at first. One day, a client said casually "This time, we have to be just a little careful. We can't overdo it." No one thought anything of it. Of course, photographers took the slightly less-padded assignments

—even though watching their expenses was a new experience.

In the sixties and the seventies, affluence had shaped the culture. Much of Kane's pictorial legacy is a reflection of a time when everything was made possible by an influx of money—everything, from the youth rebellion, which he documented through elaborate portraits of musicians and rock stars, to the sexual revolution, which he celebrated with provocative images of young women. Even his less commercial photographs—his photo-essays on racism, his numerous travel pictures, his lyrical photo-illustrations—were commissioned by big-budget magazines, including *Life*, *Vogue*, *Look*, and *Sports Illustrated*. But the rapidly shrinking budget was not the only phenomenon challenging Kane's life and work. Much more insidious was the fact that art direction was no longer an all-boys club. A number of influential women were now shaping the visual content of magazines—and they were easily offended by the long-standing sexist attitudes of big-time photographers like Kane. "He didn't know he was a male chauvinist," says Richard Kelly, who assisted Kane in the eighties. "He couldn't understand, even if you tried to explain it to him." Kelly remembers having lunch in Paris with Art Kane, Bert Stern, and David Bailey. "They were talking about the good old days, the money, the women. It was unreal. Even I was offended."

Kane's photographs of women are not as shocking today as they were a decade ago. Compared with some of the overtly degrading images of women in the latest fashion magazines, Kane's unapologetic delight in the female body is surprisingly refreshing. It's a throwback to a time when teenage girls didn't starve themselves in order to look like models, when the *Sports Illustrated* swimsuit issue was not a cynical marketing event, and when violence and sex were not one and the same. "It's cool," exclaimed a young photographer who recently stumbled on *Paper Dolls* (Grove Press), a book of Kane's most memorable erotic pictures. He had never seen such poetic images of women.

Kane could have weathered his own chauvinism if his work

had been more introspective, but he was so successful for so long that he never felt the urge to create images that had no commercial value. "Dad was too busy to do personal work," explains Jonathan, "and his photographs were so profoundly editorial, he never even tried to have a gallery show." Photographer Duane Michals, who always admired Kane's flamboyant style, believes that Kane didn't consider himself an artist, "probably because he never found that private and intimate part of his work."

So, when the money began to dry up and the "new" (read "female") generation of art directors moved in, Kane was caught off-guard. Still a superstar in Europe, where he incarnated the American Dream, he faded into oblivion at home. "For a long time, Kane was an extraordinary prodigy, always exceptional," says Milton Glaser. "He was a glamour figure in the graphic arts. He could do no wrong." But the very people he had loved and celebrated all his life—young women—were now changing the editorial design field and shunning men like him who didn't support their sensibility. "Like so many of us, he was unprepared for the second half of his life," adds Glaser. "He had nothing to fall back on—no friendships, only ex-wives."

But Kane could always fall back on his gift for storytelling. No one could take that away from him. He didn't care what he did, where he went, or who he saw—as long as he could get a yarn out of it. "Whenever we traveled together on assignments," remembers Richard Kelly, "there was always a great story to be told after the trip. Art saw humor in everything." True to form, at the end of his life, Art Kane got to tell his best tale ever—the story of his "first" picture. In 1958, when he was working as an art director at an agency, Robert Benton, then at *Esquire*, gave him his first photo assignment: a cover story on the golden age of jazz. Kane, who claimed he had never held a camera in his hands before, accepted the challenge. He ended up shooting four photographs, all memorable: Louis Armstrong sitting in a rocking chair in Death Valley, a distorted reflection of Lester

Young, a picture of Charlie Parker's open sax case next to his grave, and a group portrait of 57 of New York's jazz greats. This last picture, which, for the sake of the story, Kane said was his first ever, is the one that was to propel him back into the limelight more than three decades later, when Jean Bach made a film about it.

"No one knows exactly how the word got out in Harlem that *Esquire* was planning to take a group shot of jazz musicians," says Bach, 80. "But the magazine had connections, and Kane was a very hyper young man who made things happen." So, incredibly, such night creatures as Thelonious Monk, Count Basie, Dizzie Gillespie, Lester Young, Roy Eldridge, and Charles Mingus showed up at about ten in the morning in front of an old brownstone on 126th Street. Everyone was surprised to see so many people turn out. One musician said that "he wasn't aware there were two ten o'clocks in the same day." The atmosphere on the street was that of a class reunion, with musicians embracing each other and catching up, while Kane, perched on a stoop across the street, tried desperately to get them to line up for a shot.

Mona Hinton, married to bassist Milt Hinton, had brought an 8-mm color camera and took a home movie of that glorious morning. When, in the early nineties, Jean Bach began to research the history of the photograph, she discovered the makings of a great documentary. With interviews of Kane and of surviving musicians mixed in with footage from the handheld film, snapshots taken by friends, and outtakes of jazz performances, she brought the excitement of that day back to life. Nominated for an Academy Award in 1995 for best documentary, her film showcased Art Kane's humor, his quick wit, his natural charm—and his talent for creating unforgettable images.

One week after *A Great Day in Harlem* was nominated, Kane decided that as far as he was concerned, his narrative was complete. Although he had been manic depressive for years, he had somehow learned to function in spite of his illness. "As always," says Jonathan, "his timing was impeccable. The film was a success, the time was right." In a brutal gesture that horrified his friends, but did not shock them, Kane put a gun to his head and ended his life.

His obituary in *The New York Times* identified him only as the photographer of the Harlem picture. "If he wasn't dead already," says Jean Bach "that would have killed him. No one cared to remember all his subsequent work, yet he had tons of great stuff." The photograph for which he is most remembered is but one of his thousand-word pictures.

Who owns images?
In theory, if you create a work of art,
you own it. But more and more
illustrators today sign contracts that give
clients complete control of their
images—including the right to silkscreen
them on the surface of Mars!

21

Today, illustrators are plagued by stagnant fees, onerous contracts, and copycats willing to plagiarize their style and sell their bad imitations for stock. Yet polite outrage is all these talented artists express when they talk about their predicament. Case in point: A busy illustrator who must supplement her income by moonlighting as an art director. When asked how much she thinks would be fair market value for her illustration work, she only gives herself a 20 percent raise—a modest sum, considering that she only keeps half of her fees after commissions and taxes.

"I know what goes into doing an illustration," I tell her. "It's not just the craft, it's also the ability to think and visualize abstractions. What the heck! I believe that, all things considered, you should demand at least three times that amount."

She is not amused. "Why would I do that? I would never get it. What's the use of overpricing yourself?"

Hold it! I was just speculating. I too gave up my day job to embrace the life of a freelance writer. Although my name is often credited on the top of the page, I am well aware that I am at the bottom of the food chain. "I know what you mean," I say, conciliatory. "We artists sign our work, but we hardly get rewarded for it."

She agrees. To make ends meet, illustrators must deliver at least five spot illustrations a week. "We are often faced with crushing deadlines," she explains. "But we are afraid to turn down work for fear of losing clients."

Today, illustrators take for granted that they are lucky to eke out a living. It didn't used to be that way. In the 1930s, in the middle of the Depression, a cover by the likes of Norman Rockwell fetched $8,000; a full-page illustration was $2,000—enough money for a down payment on a house. Today, more than 60 years later, the going rate is half as much, not taking inflation into account. Illustrators are the victims of one of the worst wage depreciations in history.

Though there is, at long last, a growing awareness of how

unfair this situation is, too few illustrators believe that they are in a position to negotiate higher fees—even top New York talents like Steve Brodner or Istvan Banyai. Brodner, who averages three to four illustrations a week, says: "I work very hard to support my family. I only want to get what's fair. I don't want conflict." Says Banyai: "I do about 120 major illustrations a year, not counting books. I work all the time. I never go out with other illustrators: We are a boring bunch—all we do is complain about fees, but we don't do a thing about it."

Illustrators are not known for their ability to organize. They are loners who would rather work in their studio than attend meetings. "When we get together, we talk about philosophy," says New York illustrator Guy Billout. "The money issues are too painful or too messy."

According to Teresa Shelley from Reilly Illustration, a New York agency that represents such legendary illustrators as Jean Jacques Sempé, Edward Koren, Pierre Le-Tan, and Philippe Weisbecker, there is plenty of money around, "but it never seeps down to the level of the artist. A house painter painting a white wall makes more money than an illustrator."

The situation is no better in Europe, says Philippe Arnaud, who represents 20 artists, including Jean-Philippe Delhomme and André François. "Big advertisers will try to drive fees down as far as possible," says Arnaud, "but I refuse to work with them unless they are willing to pay the price to maintain the market value of my artists' ego."

Well said. It's about time someone speaks up in defense of illustrators' egos, since they won't do it themselves. But turning down jobs that pay too little is tougher on artists than on their agents. Not surprisingly, a number of Arnaud's illustrators are economically challenged: The price of maintaining the market value of their ego is an address on the wrong side of town.

The cost of an original illustration is minimal compared with the cost of a photo shoot. Yet, because illustrations are considered the cheaper alternative, only a handful of art directors have enough clout to convince their corporate clients that an established illustrator deserves what he or she asks for. And with art schools flooding the market with a steady supply of eager young illustrators, there is no shortage of new talent. "There are too many kids willing to work for free," says illustrator Mirko Ilic, former art director of *The New York Times* op-ed page. "But it's our fault. We don't educate young people to stand up for their rights. We painted ourselves in a corner—and corporate America was much too happy to provide the paint."

Although more sympathetic to artists, editorial art directors are just as opportunistic. Even the most prestigious illustration-driven magazines can't resist capitalizing on the illustrators' eagerness to see their work in print. Art director Judy Garland, who did so much to promote good illustration at *The Atlantic Monthly* concedes: "I feel so guilty—our prices haven't changed in almost two decades."

"Most people are really excited to get an assignment from us," says Gail Anderson, deputy art director at *Rolling Stone*. "We trust each other. I give them complete freedom. Sometimes we chat on the phone for hours. It's a wonderful relationship, except that I wish I could push the fees up a bit."

One of the most lucrative illustration assignments in the editorial world is a cover for *Time* magazine—where fees climb as high as $5,000. But you must do it overnight. Gone are the days when artists were given a six-week lead time and when a successful illustrator did 20 illustrations a year. "Today, working more is the only way to make more money," says Tim O'Brien, a New York illustrator. His yearly average? Sixty pieces: five major illustrations a month, no vacations.

"The most frightening trend is not low fees," says Paul Basista, former director of the Graphic Artists Guild, a professional association dedicated to improving the situation for its members and actively promoting a change of attitude. As he explains, being underpaid is the least of the problems illustrators face today. "There is a concerted, deliberate, and cynical effort by those in control of the media to steal from illustrators," he says. "Corporations offer work-for-hire contracts to illustrators in order to amass a library of images they hope to reuse later for huge profits when the Web is no longer free."

In theory, if you create a work of art, you own it. But in fact, more and more illustrators today sign contracts that "hereby irrevocably assigns all rights, title, and interest in and to the work, and all copyrights related hereby, to the company." Accordingly, and I quote, "the client has the right to publish, create derivative work from, use, adapt, edit, modify, or reproduce in any form or media whatsoever, or to transfer or license any rights or derivations thereof to third parties, no matter how many times the work is published, in any form or media."

In other words, the spot illustration you did last week could turn up in ten years as a billboard on Mars! Although your name may appear on it—to add some old-fashioned cachet to the design—the colors, proportions, and cropping could be different. Parts could be redrawn while others may be blurred, distorted, textured, sharpened, or enlarged. "Yes, they have the right to do that too," says O'Brien. "If they buy the copyright on your piece, they can change it." And of course, you get no residuals from it.

When the Graphic Artists Guild and the Society of Illustrators come together to examine the situation, as they have in the past, their approach is conciliatory. They are not about to bite the hand that feeds them. "You can initiate a dialogue by crossing out items in a contract," says Brodner, who spearheaded a committee to educate illustrators on their rights. "Before threatening to go to court, try guilt. You'll be surprised: Along the line of power, there are places where moral people make moral judgments."

Some illustrators would love to beat their corporate clients at their own game. Seymour Chwast of Pushpin fame is among them. He recycles his old illustrations and turns them into royalty-free images. Digitized and sold on CD-ROMs, the art goes into the public domain. "I have done so many spot illustrations, sometimes I don't even remember doing them," says mild-mannered Chwast. "I wouldn't put on these disks work I feel very close to because, once I release them, I have no control over how they are manipulated. Anyway, my name doesn't go on them."

This cavalier attitude toward art makes some fellow illustrators very nervous, to say the least. "He is helping destroy illustration," says Ilic, who sees clip art as the commodification of creativity. That's much too dramatic a statement for mischievous Chwast, who says that his disks are only moderately successful anyway. "Once, I used one of my own illustrations from one of my disks, and I liked the result," he adds with no false modesty.

Also ahead of the selling-out curve are illustrators who sit down to create from scratch ready-to-go, plug-and-play stock illustration. "It takes a special person to create what I call a universal style," says Marie-Christine Matter, who created the Stock Illustration Source, probably the biggest stock illustration agency in the world with a large share of the market in the United States, England, Germany, Italy, and Japan. That special person, most people agree, is a bad illustrator.

In the SIS catalogue, more than 15,000 illustrations are indexed with more the 40,000 key words. Magritte-inspired visual metaphors are best-sellers: globes, bridges, cliffs, clouds, lightbulbs, ladders, arrows, question marks, and more globes—reflecting the concern of a global economy desperately trying to keep up with changes.

Although the artists' names in stock illustrations must appear next to the work, their style is so derivative it might as well be anonymous. Every month, all around the world, illustrators who imitate the technique of Brad Holland, Michel Folon, or Henrik Drescher get fat checks from stock houses. "Brad Holland is probably the most copied illustrator in the world," says Mark Helfin, who edits the *American Illustration* series. "It really hurts him. Anyone can get a badly designed, fake Brad

Holland for a fraction of what he would charge."

There are no regulations in stock illustration, and it is here to stay. "It's a brilliant idea commercially," says illustrator Guy Billout, who put a half-dozen of his illustrations on consignment with SIS and is now sorry he did. "It's like self-service for art directors. There is no vision, only mediocrity."

The painful issue of who owns an image obscures the real issue: Who should take credit for the message encrypted in an illustration? "Illustrators have such great minds," says Elisabeth Biondi, visuals director at *The New Yorker*. "Their images are like fiction—they augment the text." A former picture editor at *Vanity Fair* and *Stern*, Biondi is a strong advocate of photography, yet she often finds herself preferring drawings to photographs to illustrate a *New Yorker* piece. "Illustrators come up with images that both entice and surprise the readership," she says.

Maybe illustrators work too hard. They are losing sight of the fact that their creations are not objects to sell, but intellectual property. To reclaim their rights, they would do well to shed their *artiste* persona and reposition themselves as authors—as equal partners of the storytelling process. There are some hopeful signs—the increasing popularity of animation, the growth of children's literature—indications that some illustrators are no longer willing to simply embellish the page. They've realized that asserting their authorship is the only way to transcend the conundrum of ownership.

Object lesson #3: the car
Today it takes a car, not a man, to make
a woman out of a girl! When my daughter
was in her preteens, she started to ask
me a lot of embarrassing questions about
my driving, such as, "Mom, do you
know how to downshift?"

22

A friend of mine had decided to put her career on hold for a while and have a child. She proudly announced her intentions to her loved ones, and to celebrate, she took a day off from work in the middle of the week. That morning she went for a brisk walk and soon found herself in the part of town where car dealerships spangle their premises in tinsel as if to attract swallows. Feeling as free as a bird, she, too, started to soar. Two hours later she was driving a little red Miata off the Mazda lot.

With the motor purring at her knees and the road stretching deliciously at her feet, the mother-to-be, now in fifth gear, rolled down the windows and leaned her elbow into the wind. She drove all afternoon, until nightfall, and when at last she parked her new car in front of her house, she had traveled much farther than the 100 miles tallied on the odometer. Sometimes you have to go quite a distance just to catch up with yourself: the "baby" she had been dreaming about, she realized, had a four-cylinder, 16-valve, double overhead-cam engine and looked like a Lotus Elan from the Sixties.

Women and cars are a powerful match: Each propelled by a fierce and invisible inner drive, they are suited to each other for reasons more emotional than mechanical. Together they are a modern version of a centaur, which in this new incarnation has bosom and wheels instead of the traditional male torso and equine legs—a heroic and skittish animal, one equally responsive to the laws of thermodynamics and to the absurdities of love. The surprising affinity between these two unlikely partners—one is supposed to be soft, the other hard—comes from the fact that, undaunted by technological expertise, women are more likely to think of cars as people, or at least as personalities. They equate the possession of a vehicle with something as emotionally demanding, and as emotionally fulfilling, as a relationship. The fair sex will put up with a lot of hassle and aggravation in exchange for protection and physical closeness, and such mutual trust and intimacy are exactly what we instinctively acknowledge when we get into a car and close the door.

Today it takes a car, not a man, to make a woman out of a girl! When my daughter was in her preteens, she started to ask me a lot of embarrassing questions about my driving, such as, "Mom, do you know how to downshift?" During her puberty we often talked about speed limits, left-hand turns, and parallel parking as if we were sharing some confidential and very personal information. As expected, the first time she borrowed my car for the evening, I checked it over as if it were her date. Then resigned, I watched my babies drive away.

The next day when she returned the keys, she mentioned casually that there was a funny noise in the muffler, and that the transmission was starting to slip—an innocent way of establishing her new territory and sharing it with me. I promised to look into it, but I did not tell her that first I had to look into myself, and accept the fact that from now on there was another woman in the house. I checked my jealousy and figured that my job as a mother was to nurture the woman as much as I had nurtured the girl. Expressions like "Mom, you need an oil change" or "your back tires are low" were manifestations of her growing independence, and a chance for me to encourage her in that direction. Every Saturday she would wash the car with the same care and command she had displayed when she was grooming her horse. Unsentimental, businesslike, but fully engaged, she would give the hubcaps a final brisk polish. "Mom, I bought a new air filter," she said one day—and then I realized that what turns a girl into a woman is not the car but its maintenance.

A driving passion runs in the family. A real *grande dame*, my mother drives the way she lives, with a glint in her eyes; she solves traffic dilemmas with the gas pedal, not the brakes. One day, years ago, I foolishly offered to take her to the train station when she was returning to Paris after a short visit to Chamonix, where I was vacationing with my new American husband. With a fresh New York State driver's license tucked into my French passport, I stowed her bags in the trunk of the rented car, made sure she was comfortably seated next to me, and took to the road with casual self-assurance, forgetting I was in France, not in the United States.

More trucks than we had expected were slowly negotiating the mountainous curves. I grew slightly nervous as my mother grew impatient. I could tell she wanted to take the wheel and show me how to deal with the situation, but there was not room on either side of the switchback road for me to safely pull over. I pressed on with sweaty palms, trying to pass the lumbering giants. At one point, when I was tentatively evaluating my chances of overtaking a colossal rig, I heard my mother's voice ring in my ears. "Just go," she ordered, "go now!" My blood—her blood—curdled in my veins. To die and be worthy of her grit, or to live forever as a wimp: these were my only options. I raced past the mass of roaring metal in what was indeed a rite of passage.

I admire the healthy and confident way that American women relate to their cars. From my girlfriend in Nantucket, who drives a bulky 1951 Ford station wagon on the dirt roads and cobblestone streets of the island as if it were an off-road vehicle, to her sister in Los Angeles, who practically lives on the Santa Monica Freeway in her diesel Mercedes, surrounded by portable infant car seats, screaming toddlers, and bags of groceries, every single female car owner in this country is a study in style and cool efficiency. The thrill of this discovery is a never-ending source of pleasure: a wiry girl in a summer dress who casually changed the oil in her Peugeot at a bus stop in New Mexico, an old lady in the Napa Valley who jump-started my car from her orange Volkswagen bug, an independently wealthy young woman who drove a Bentley but lived in a log cabin in Wyoming—all of them loom large in the rearview mirror of my memory. With each encounter, exotic and magical because of its friendly randomness, I realize how far I have journeyed since I left Paris, a city that seems, in comparison, like a safe and provincial spot on the map.

In most European towns, cars are the natural predator of

pedestrians. At the crosswalks they rev their engines and growl at your ankles. They belch fumes in your face. They ambush from hidden drives. Sometimes the driver even sticks his head out the side window and whistles or, worse, voices his unsolicited opinion about your figure, your hairstyle, and the length of your skirt.

Perhaps women abroad are fastidiously chic just to goad the automotive industry, which has been historically unsympathetic to the needs of their fashion-minded customers. Whereas early car designers were aware that the bottom part of an outfit is just as delicate as its top, and thus gave women plenty of room below the waist, later models forced women to give up their voluminous skirts. The introduction of the slick and slinky Citroën DS in 1955 heralded the end of true elegance in France. How can you dress properly and then stuff yourself into a compact sedan? In the early 1950s, before the demise of roomy cars, my father drove his four teenage daughters to visit his mother on weekends; he had no problem finding a model large enough to accommodate four Brigitte Bardot skirts with seriously starched petticoats. But when his old Traction Avant (Big 15) had to be retired, we gave up our Sunday drives and took the subway to our grandmother's apartment near the Eiffel Tower. Anyway, the New Look and its flaring and flouncing skirts had run its course. We were now riding the A line.

Moving to New York City in the 1960s somewhat eased my relationship with cars, although in many ways Manhattan is nothing but another European town. Only Cadillacs had the power to disorient and captivate me; they combined the aesthetics of Cuban nightclubs (embroidered-leather seats and gold trim) with decorative elements characteristic of hotel lobbies (luxurious ashtrays and copper-finished lighting fixtures). Attempting to become a native, I bought a white Chevrolet Camaro in the early 1970s. Now I only remember driving it endlessly around the Upper East Side in pursuit of a parking spot. Toward the end of that decade I purchased a red 1953 Ford pickup truck to try my hand at yet another American cliché. I loved cruising around New York perched four feet above the traffic, and parking in the yellow zones as if I were making a delivery. A couple of times I took it to black-tie events at the Waldorf-Astoria or the Plaza, and had fun dropping it off casually for valet parking. To me, satin and chrome, velvet and a flatbed, pearls and running boards were irresistible and glamorous combinations.

But despite my efforts to embrace the concept, I was still far from understanding this American experience—wheels. In the 1980s, I settled finally in California, where I encountered the authentic car culture; for the first time I got a chance to pump my own gas. An enthusiastic explorer of the American way of life, I looked forward to the Western freeway as yet another installment in a series of picturesque discoveries. But nothing could have prepared me for the inescapable euphoria I experienced when I hit the gas pedal and felt the smooth asphalt under me. No one had warned me that in the West, to go is to arrive, and that the open road is the end of the journey. By the time I figured it out, it was too late; I was addicted. In this new form of happiness I found a delicious finality and thus a very existential—and very French—sense of desperation.

I traveled the farthest away from home—home was still a pair of high-heeled red satin sandals I had bought in 1973 at the Yves Saint Laurent boutique in Paris—the day I pulled up at a filling station on a dusty stretch of highway on the outskirts of San Jose, in Silicon Valley. It was a self-service pump, and you had to walk to the tin-roofed convenience store to pay for the gas. As was often the case in those days, I affectionately noted the row of tall emaciated palm trees hanging at the edge of the lot, the neon signs, the lanky truck drivers going to and fro. How could a setup so foreign to me be so keenly familiar? As I shoved the gas nozzle into the car, keeping the hose wrapped around my right leg to prevent the perverse contraption from jerking about, the vile smell of gasoline came rushing at me. Instead of turning away from it, as I had done all my life, I inhaled deeply.

Benzine, butane, isooctane—barbaric names with organic roots, and with the power to stimulate the mind. The fumes reeked of life, a life so malodorous it was still evolving. For one horrifying second, I felt as if I were pumping the very essence of Deep Time into my car. And then I inhaled once more to fix forever in my olfactory memory the pungency of my new emancipation.

Although stowed away under the hood, the engineering of a car is immediately palpable to a woman the minute she sits down and puts her hands on the steering wheel. The finely tuned instruments, like well-tailored garments, appeal to her femininity. In fact, the automobile lost some of its "boyness" when its mechanisms became so meticulously balanced with vacuum hoses that the average American male could no longer take it apart and put it back together in the family garage as he had for generations; now he had to take it to the shop for repairs. Japanese engineering has done more for women's liberation than the Pill. Now the fair sex is just as likely to appreciate the acceleration rate of a vehicle, the way it handles on the road, the smoothness and coordination of gestures required to shift gears, as any man ever did. The smell of a new car is not a gender-selective stimulant; it stirs some elemental craving in every member of the species. You get in and close the door; instinctively you inhale and your soul expands; your hands reach for the belt and you buckle up; you relax—bound together, flesh and metal now feel invincible.

With the feminization of technology and the latest engineering advances in the automotive industry, manufacturers are becoming more subtle and sophisticated, and are now expressing subjective feelings toward cars with some poetic license—headlights with batting eyelids, dashboards that speak to you in languid voices, seats that can massage your back. My Honda has a security system that's moody and temperamental, and sometimes I have to plead and coax before I am allowed to open the door. I don't mind the courtship. Cars used to be promiscuous; now they are worldly, quietly sensual, and require from us a different kind of commitment.

One spring day, after a sedentary winter, I decided to drive straight from New York City to Atlanta just to give myself the kind of spiritual stretch that comes from miles spent on the road inside a vehicle whose only destination is the sunset. With nowhere to go but the next rest stop on the thruway, I get closer to the land I was supposedly in such a hurry to put behind me. Nature was in full bloom, and the roadside was a lush jungle of fresh greens—a sharp contrast to the fiery urgency of my aimless journey. Did I feel guilty? No, I reasoned, the burned asphalt is the price one pays to contemplate the beauty of creation. To leave the car in the garage and forgo such a spectacle would be criminally negligent.

Inspired, I stopped at a scenic overlook with a view of the Blue Ridge Mountains, where an electrical storm was gathering its stage magic. I got out to stretch and yawn. The car, sounding now like an ice cube popping in a tall drink, was doing a little cooling off of its own. Its gasoline breath, blending with the scent of new grass and ozone in the air, was comforting. I measured how far I had traveled with the machine. Could I have driven 1,000 miles to come a couple of inches closer to an inner perception of what my life is about? Yes. A car is only a means of transportation, but it's designed to take you in just one direction: forward.